New Library of Pastoral Care

Letting Go

New Library of Pastoral Care

STILL SMALL VOICE
An Introduction to Pastoral
Counselling
Michael Jacobs

MAKE OR BREAK
An Introduction to Marriage
Counselling
Jack Dominian

SWIFT TO HEAR
Facilitating Skills in Listening
and Responding
Michael Jacobs

BRIEF ENCOUNTERS
Pastoral Ministry through Baptisms,
Weddings and Funerals
Wesley Carr

LOVE THE STRANGER
Ministry in Multi-Faith Areas
Roger Hooker and Christopher Lamb

BEING THERE
Care in Time of Illness
Peter Speck

CRISIS COUNSELLING
Caring for People in Emotional
Shock
Howard Stone

LIFE CYCLES
Women and Pastoral Care
*Elaine Graham and
Margaret Halsey (eds)*

GOING SOMEWHERE
People with Mental Handicaps and
their Pastoral Care
Sheila Hollins and Margaret Grimer

MADE IN HEAVEN?
Ministry with Those Intending
Marriage
Peter Chambers

HELPING THE HELPERS
Supervision and Pastoral Care
John Foskett and David Lyall

CLERGY STRESS
The Hidden Conflicts in Ministry
Mary Anne Coate

HOLDING IN TRUST
The Appraisal of Ministry
Michael Jacobs

BEING YOUR AGE
Pastoral Care for Older People
Michael Butler and Ann Orbach

SIN, GUILT AND FORGIVENESS
The Hidden Dimensions of a Pastoral
Process
Mary Anne Coate

SOCIOLOGY FOR PASTORAL
CARE
George Furniss

A DICTIONARY OF
PASTORAL CARE
edited by Alastair V. Campbell

NEW·LIBRARY·OF

PASTORAL·CARE

LETTING GO

Caring for the Dying and the Bereaved

Ian Ainsworth-Smith
and Peter Speck

SPCK

First published 1982
SPCK
Holy Trinity Church
Marylebone Road
London NW1 4DU

New edition 1999

British Library Cataloguing-in-Publication Data

A catalogue record for this book is available
from the British Library

ISBN 0-281-05225-5

Typeset by Pioneer Associates, Perthshire
Printed in Great Britain by
The Cromwell Press, Trowbridge, Wiltshire

Contents

	Foreword	vii
	Introduction	ix
	Acknowledgements	x
1	Opportunity for Growth – Facing the Death of Another	1
2	Opportunity for Growth – Facing our own Death	18
3	Letting Go	39
4	The Context of Dying	50
5	Rites and Customs	70
6	When Grief Goes Wrong	119
7	Focus on the Minister	129
	Appendix A: Practicalities	147
	Appendix B: Useful Addresses	155
	Appendix C: Some Other Cultural Patterns	157
	Select Bibliography	162
	Index	164

To all those people, living and departed, who have assisted our understanding in many different ways

Foreword

The *New Library of Pastoral Care* has been planned to meet the needs of those people concerned with pastoral care, whether clergy or lay, who seek to improve their knowledge and skills in this field. Equally, it is hoped that it may prove useful to those secular helpers who may wish to understand the role of the pastor.

Pastoral care in every age has drawn from contemporary secular knowledge to inform its understanding of men and women and their various needs and of the ways in which these needs might be met. Today it is perhaps the secular helping professions of social work, counselling and psychotherapy, and community development which have particular contributions to make to pastors in their work. Such knowledge does not stand still, and pastors would have a struggle to keep up with the endless tide of new developments which pour out from these and other disciplines, and to sort out which ideas and practices might be relevant to their particular pastoral needs. Among present-day ideas, for instance, of particular value might be an understanding of the social context of the pastoral task, the dynamics of the helping relationship, the attitudes and skills as well as factual knowledge which might make for effective pastoral intervention, and perhaps most significant of all, the study of particular cases, whether through verbatim reports of interviews or general case presentation. The discovery of ways of learning from what one is doing is becoming increasingly important.

There is always a danger that a pastor who drinks deeply at the well of a secular discipline may lose their grasp of their own pastoral identity and become 'just another' social worker or counsellor. It in no way detracts from the value of these professions to assert that the role and task of the pastor are quite unique among the helping professions and deserve to be clarified and strengthened rather than weakened. The theological commitment of the pastor and the appropriate use of their role are recurrent themes of this series. At the same time the pastor cannot afford to work in a vacuum. They need to be able to communicate and co-operate with those helpers in other disciplines whose work may overlap, without loss of their own unique role. This in turn will mean being able to communicate with them through some understanding of their concepts and language.

Finally, there is a rich variety of styles and approaches in pastoral work within the various religious traditions. No attempt is made to secure a uniform approach. The Library will contain the variety, and even perhaps occasional eccentricity, which such a title suggests. Some books will be more specifically theological and others more concerned with particular areas of need or practice. It is hoped that all of them will have a usefulness that will reach right across the boundaries of religious denomination.

Introduction to the Second Edition

Since the first edition of this book the number of publications concerned with dying and bereaved people has reached almost avalanche proportions. A few of these books specifically address the pastoral issues of caring for those who are dying or bereaved. We believe that *Letting Go* holds a central place within the pastoral literature and that this second edition will remain a valuable practical text for ministers of religion and students in training.

Many people, in various parts of the world, have expanded the knowledge of bereavement and terminal care through extensive research and the development of new models of care. The hospice movement has engendered a more widely applied understanding of palliative care, both in its general form in hospitals, community and primary care, and within more specialist palliative care services as defined by the National Hospices Council. This revised edition of *Letting Go* reflects these developments and the recognition of a more truly multi-professional approach to care. It is even more important today that all in ministry develop a good grasp of the newer understandings and models of grief, while retaining their own identity as the 'holy person' often within a secular setting. Without clarity of vision on these issues it will be difficult for the pastor to develop a clear understanding of his/her specific contribution to the multi-professional approach.

The authors continue to work within health care chaplaincy and so the text reflects our own experience of working with dying and bereaved people and those who care for them. The stories referred to in the text are reproduced with the subjects' permission, or that of their family, or have been made anonymous to protect confidentiality.

We are both priests within the Anglican tradition but believe the text is applicable to all who exercise a pastoral role, whether clergy or lay. We hope readers will continue to benefit from this sharing of our insight and experience, and will develop the practice of reflecting on their own, and that this will enhance their own understanding and pastoral care.

Peter Speck
Ian Ainsworth-Smith

Autumn 1998

ACKNOWLEDGEMENTS

We are indebted to a growing number of people as the years pass. To those who have shared their stories with us – often painfully. To our own families and colleagues who have supported us, helped in researching material, and provided valuable criticism and advice on both the old and the new text.

We also acknowledge our indebtedness to the late Canon Norman Autton whose inspired texts in the original Library of Pastoral Care were as formative for us as they were for many other hospital chaplains and parish clergy over the years.

Acknowledgement is also due to the following for permission to quote from published sources: D. Reidel Publishing Company, for extracts from 'A Time to Live, A Time to Grieve' by Janice Reid, first published in *Culture, Medicine and Psychiatry* 3 (1979); The Consumers' Association, for the table from *What to Do When Someone Dies* by P. Harris (1998); The Stationery Office, for the table 'Ways in which Family and Friends Helped the Bereaved after the Death', from *Families, Funerals and Finances* by P. J. Hennessy (1980); Colin Murray Parkes for permission to adapt and use his diagram on page 126.

ONE

Opportunity for Growth – Facing the Death of Another

He that conceals his grief finds
no remedy for it. (Turkish Proverb)

The death of someone you know and love can be a devastating experience in which a large part of your world is lost. The process by which we seek to fill the gap in our lives and to find a new equilibrium is described as grief.

Sorrow is an essential ingredient of grief with an associated pining for the world that has been lost, rather than for the object itself. It is as if an important 'point of reference' has disappeared in our lives and we are adrift until we can establish new landmarks. To describe grief as a process rightly implies that we are thinking of something occurring over a period of time, and that its nature will change with time.

Grief seems to run a more or less constant course but its expression may be modified by various factors. The abruptness of the loss and the opportunity given to us to prepare for the loss are important. The nature of the relationship between the bereaved and the deceased as well as the previous personality of the bereaved are also significant factors. Clearly the death of a much loved husband will evoke a different response from that consequent upon the death of a distant uncle whom you never really liked. The ambivalence that exists in many of our relationships can greatly influence our reactions in the presence of death.

Sometimes the grief experience will enable us to use the time to grow closer to those who are around us, but for some it has the opposite effect in that it isolates and seems to push us away from other people. In a similar way people may either grow closer to God or alienate themselves from him when they are faced with such a crisis. A person will sometimes say, 'I just cannot believe in a God who lets such things happen. My faith has been shattered.' The opportunity for growth is there, but we may not always be able to grasp it. The role of those who are around the dying and the bereaved would seem to be that of giving the other person the *full right* to feel and express his or her own feelings and thus enable growth to take place. 'He that conceals his grief finds no remedy for it.' If we are to enable people to work through their grief then we need to understand and recognize some of the reactions that may be experienced as we face the reality of death and bereavement.

Craig Jenkins was six years of age when he had his accident. His 12-year-old brother (Wayne) had recently had a new bike and Craig had pestered him constantly to let him ride it, although it was too big for him. Because of the way Craig always seemed to mess up his brother's things Wayne had said no. One day after school, before his brother arrived home, Craig took the bike out of the shed and set off down the road, without telling his mother. At the corner he failed to stop and went straight into the path of a passing van. Craig sustained severe head injuries and was rushed to hospital. The bike was ruined.

A neighbour ran to tell Craig's family what had happened and Mrs Jenkins went to the hospital where her husband later joined her.

At the hospital Craig was admitted to the Neurosurgery Unit and his parents 'moved in'. The nursing staff, while acknowledging their distress, found Craig's parents quite difficult to support. They surrounded Craig with toys and brought in a portable television and cassette recorder to stimulate him into some response, in spite of being told that he was deeply unconscious. Whenever staff requested peace and quiet, or that the parents should have a break and go for a walk, a meal, or some rest, they became very aggressive and accused staff of trying to get rid of them, but 'they knew their rights'. Meanwhile the 16-year-old daughter, who had just started work, was left to look after the house and the 12-year-old brother.

The local vicar heard of the accident and visited the hospital to see what was happening. Craig's mother looked apprehensive to see the vicar, but before he could say very much Craig's father told him to clear off. 'There's nothing you can say to me. What sort of God could stand back and let a kid suffer like this. You'd better go before I say or do something I shouldn't.' The vicar said that he would leave, but that he would keep in touch, that he understood Mr Jenkins's anger and if they wished would be willing to talk to them later when they calmed down. He added that they would pray for Craig in church. As the vicar left the ward, Mrs Jenkins followed him and said, 'I've only got a minute or I'll be in trouble, but thanks for coming. It gave me a shock to see you at first. I thought the staff had called you and that Craig was dying, but I know he will be all right. Craig always says his prayers at night, say one for him please.' With that she turned round quickly and went off in search of a toilet, where she could cry alone.

Craig's condition remained critical for several days and the parents stayed at the hospital only leaving the bedside alternately so that someone was always with him in case he woke up.

On the fourth day the staff suggested that the parents go together to the canteen for some food or a break. Mrs Jenkins thought that a good idea and eventually her husband agreed provided the cassette recorder was left on while they were away. Twenty minutes after they had left the ward Craig died. The parents were very distressed and Mr Jenkins became very abusive and aggressive towards the staff nurse who had suggested they leave the ward. His wife meanwhile was oblivious to this and sat holding Craig and talking to him as if he were still alive. She seemed completely dazed and unable to take in that he had died. Then she began to cry and sat in the chair rocking to and fro saying, 'Why, why, why?' One of the nursing staff stood next to her with her arm around Mrs Jenkins. Mr Jenkins, having vented his wrath, came across to his wife. He touched his son on the head, then kissed his forehead and, turning to his wife, said, 'He's gone to sleep. Say goodnight and come home.' When they reached home and started to explain to their family what had happened the reality of the death began to sink in.

The vicar was contacted about the funeral. When he visited the family he found that the front room of the house had been cleared of all furniture and that Craig's coffin was in the centre of the room surrounded by toys. Mr Jenkins was clearly very ambivalent about the vicar (as was the vicar about Mr Jenkins!) but Mrs Jenkins seemed to see him as an ally who understood how she felt. Wayne (the 12-year-old brother) was very withdrawn and would not go into the front room or talk to anyone about Craig. He stayed upstairs most of the time, watching television. It was assumed that he would not attend the funeral, but on the day he came downstairs dressed ready to go and silently got into the car. A lot of people attended the funeral and there were masses of flowers. After the funeral Mrs Jenkins talked of 'having lost her baby', and several people advised her to 'get pregnant, it's the best thing'. Craig's part of the bedroom was kept as if he were expected home – a shrine. His brother, who shared the bedroom, became very disturbed and got into trouble for shoplifting and vandalism. Mr Jenkins seemed to get very angry with his wife and to drink quite a bit. On one occasion he blamed her for not supervising Craig properly or checking that he could not get hold of the bike. When Mrs Jenkins became pregnant she was determined it should be a boy and that they should call him Craig. Gradually the parents were becoming estranged. Mrs Jenkins started going to church and prayed constantly that her baby would be a 'new Craig'. She felt that her husband did not understand her as well as the vicar did. The vicar was very concerned about Mrs Jenkins's attitude to the expected new baby and expressed his concern to the GP whom he knew very well, so that he could keep it in mind at her next antenatal appointment, and suggested that they worked towards a joint meeting between the GP, vicar and the Jenkins family. Eventually this meeting took place.

It was a highly emotionally charged meeting and, while it was clear that Mrs Jenkins had persuaded her husband to attend, the couple were able to share some of their feelings about Craig's death and the new baby.

It was only a beginning, but hopefully it would be the commencement of a growing together and that, instead of Craig's death pushing the family apart, they might begin to draw closer together.

Shock and disbelief

Mr and Mrs Jenkins were clearly very shocked to hear of Craig's accident and found it hard to accept that he might not recover. They seemed to say that if only they could have stimulated him sufficiently they would have proved the hospital wrong. The rest of the family almost ceased to exist as they focused all their attention on Craig, with the result that their world shrank to the size of the bed-space which he occupied. Although things were happening around them and people were explaining things to them, none of it seemed to be real or to 'connect'. Many people describe a sense of numbness: 'It's almost like living in a big ball of cotton wool.'

The shock may also present itself in a physical way, coming in waves lasting from 20 minutes to about an hour: deep sighing, lack of strength and appetite, choking sensations and breathlessness, shivering and sometimes physical pain. Grief can sometimes be a very physical thing. C. S. Lewis writes:

> No one ever told me that grief felt so like fear. I am not afraid, but the sensation is like being afraid. The same fluttering in the stomach, the same restlessness, the yawning. I keep on swallowing.[1]

Talking about the impending death or the deceased tends to bring on these feelings and so the person may avoid situations and people who may trigger them off – including clergy on occasion. With Mr and Mrs Jenkins they seemed to be defending themselves from any talk of Craig dying by the use of the cassette recorder, television and their anger.

Denial of the death, or the likelihood of death, may take several forms and may last, usually, from a few hours to about two weeks. The form which the denial takes is influenced by our previous experiences of loss and separation, as well as by cultural factors. One may find a whole range from verbal denial, 'Oh, no! It isn't true' or 'I want a second opinion' (or hospital or miracle) to incapacitation (a stunned silence) or the performance of inappropriate actions (talking to the deceased and expecting a reply). Mrs Jenkins sat holding Craig and talking to him *after he died*, before she began to cry and ask, 'Why, why, why?'

Awareness

Gradually the shock and disbelief give way to a variety of different feelings which may flow back and forth like the tide, as awareness dawns.

Crying and feelings of physical emptiness are very common at this time, though not everyone will shed tears openly. Mrs Jenkins, for example, did not wish to cry in front of her husband, but waited until she could go to the toilet and be alone.

Allowing someone to cry is different from implying that they ought to cry. We should beware of statements such as 'You'd feel a lot better if you had a good cry', which sound judgemental in that they imply we think the person is acting abnormally by not crying.

Pining. Once the death has occurred the relative may well pine for the deceased and search for them with an aimless wandering around the house, neighbourhood or hospital. Pining is often accompanied by a sense of emptiness. One lady, following a stillbirth, described herself as a Henry Moore statue with a large hollow space where her stomach should have been. Sometimes the bereaved will see or hear the deceased and they will either find this very comforting or frightening. This experience will either happen during the day or as a very vivid dream which causes upset when the person wakes up and realizes it was only a dream. One widow telephoned her minister in a very distraught state to say that she thought she must be going mad. She had just prepared supper when she heard her husband (who had died two months before) put his key in the door-lock and come in. She then *saw* him hang his coat in the hall, enter the living room and sit in his favourite chair. When she fetched his supper from the kitchen he had disappeared. She screamed and dropped the meal. She needed a great deal of reassurance from her minister that she was not going mad and that this experience was quite normal. Provided these reactions are not unduly prolonged they should not cause too much concern. However, if they become very prolonged or lead to the setting up of a shrine – as in the case of the bedroom in the Jenkins's household – then this can be an indication that people may not be progressing through their grief.

Anger is a very common part of grief for many people and there was plenty of it in evidence within the Jenkins family! This anger is frequently displaced in three directions: against medicine, against God, against the deceased or self.

Mr and Mrs Jenkins displayed quite a bit of anger towards the staff of the hospital at different times. While they were grateful to the staff for what they were doing for Craig, nevertheless they were suspicious that the hospital might 'give up' too soon and so they became angry at any attempt to make them see reality or to leave the bedside. Because many relatives feel inadequate in the face of acute illness this can lead to angry criticism of the care given by the staff, as a way of showing that the relatives care.[2] Sometimes this anger is directed at the hospital doctor (for being unable to cure), at the general practitioner (for not diagnosing the condition earlier), or the ambulance service (for the delay in collecting the patient from home).

It is likely that Craig's parents experienced, but could not express and acknowledge, aggression towards Craig himself for behaving stupidly and causing so much pain to everyone. One young father, whose wife had just delivered a stillborn child, sat holding their dead baby. He was very angry with the child and in a loud voice said to the child, 'What right had you to die when we had planned for you, wanted you and had everything ready for you?' Anger against the person who has died is often repressed because others may not understand, or may not allow us to express it. Craig's brother seemed to have a lot of repressed anger, against his brother and his parents. This was not only because of the loss of his bike but also because *his* feelings were not being acknowledged by anyone. It was his sister who eventually helped him with these feelings because she too felt similarly about the way her new job was being spoilt. She was also instrumental later in reminding her parents of the need to replace the bike, but Wayne's negative feelings had already gone deep.

Many people feel that a faith in God provides a sort of Divine Assurance Policy against anything unpleasant happening. When things do go wrong in life we may, therefore, feel that God has let us down and so we become angry with him, but try not to show it. The entry of the vicar acted as a focus for much that Mr Jenkins was feeling.

The vicar's presence in the ward served to crystallize the seriousness of Craig's condition because Mr and Mrs Jenkins were reacting to the stereotyped image of the clergy as the 'associates of undertakers', or as 'vultures' who arrive shortly before the death and whose presence may, in some strange way, actually bring about the death. To another family the arrival of a minister would be welcomed because their stereotype image might be that of a friend and a source of comfort and strength. Care is needed before using words such as 'Go forth, thou Christian soul' unless one has found out where the family are in their grief. If they are still denying the reality of impending death then these words may create fear and antipathy and the rejection of the priest's ministry. Some people who have little experience of the Church's ministry may even feel that because of the minister's authority (and 'hot-line' to God), if the words 'Go forth' are used, then the soul will. Therefore, the longer the minister is kept away the longer they can continue their pretence. Sensitivity and awareness of people's understanding of what the minister is doing are very important.

The clergy also represent God and, as in the case of Mr Jenkins, people are sometimes very angry with God for 'allowing such things to happen'. Sometimes the clergy will receive verbal, and occasionally physical, assault in such situations because the person cannot get hold of God but can get hold of the minister! Mr Jenkins was fairly restrained and simply said, 'You'd better go before I say or do something I shouldn't.' Mrs Jenkins, perhaps without realizing what she was doing, tried to placate the vicar and God and to ask him to intercede for her son's life. The way in which we cope with these angry feelings and respond to them is very important, for if we do not handle them properly they can very easily hinder growth. We shall return to this topic later.

Guilt is frequently associated with anger and is often expressed in the 'if only' questions. There is often a strong feeling in the minds of many people that there must be someone to blame for the death that has occurred or is about to occur. Therefore guilt and blame are frequently mixed in with the anger voiced against various people. Sometimes this guilt is well founded in that somebody was negligent or did contribute towards the death. We might term this *real guilt*. Real guilt is the type that one sees most frequently, where the cause and effect are clearly recognizable: the motorist who reverses his car without due care and knocks over a child; the alcoholic whose self-abuse has led to chronic liver failure; or those moments when under stress we say something very hurtful to someone else and regret it later. The fact that cause and effect may be easily identifiable does not mean that these feelings will necessarily be readily accepted.

Irrational or exaggerated guilt arises when our experience of guilt is out of all proportion to the event said to be causing it: 'If only I had made my son finish his breakfast before dashing off to school he wouldn't have been on that street corner at the time the lorry ran out of control'; or 'If only we had not had a row a month ago my husband would not be dead now'; or 'If only I had recognized earlier that he was unwell and looked after him better'. This form of guilt can sometimes lead to self-punishment in order to atone and in some way restore things to how they were. The vast array of toys with which the Jenkins family surrounded their son in hospital, and his coffin at home, seemed to be both an expression of their wanting to care, but also a means of salving their consciences for what had happened. In a similar way people may give large sums of money to the Church or to charities as a means of easing feelings of guilt in their relationship with God. One of the key roles of the clergy in respect of the guilt feelings of the bereaved is to help them to grow in their understanding of the meaning of reconciliation, forgiveness and the identification of self-punishing behaviour. In the words of Tillich, this means to foster in the person 'the courage to accept oneself as accepted in spite of being unacceptable.'[3]

This brings us to the third type of guilt which might be described as *existential guilt*. This is a nebulous area related to deeply rooted feelings of inadequacy and the acceptance of our own mortality and weaknesses. In the face of death, whether our own or that of someone else, we tend to look back over our life and reflect on words, actions and relationships and to judge ourselves according to the extent of our sense of human failure and to make excuses for it. Following the exposure of some personal failure, or its realization, existential guilt may be expressed when we excuse ourselves by saying, 'It's just the way I'm made, I can't help it.' Some guilt, therefore, is related to existence itself, to the anxiety of self-rejection and to moral self-awareness and existential doubt[4] which is often displayed in the question, 'What have I done to deserve this?' In the case of Mrs Jenkins, after the initial shock had worn off, she simply sat holding Craig and saying, 'Why, why, why?' In that Mrs Jenkins was beyond words at this time it would not have helped for the vicar to have tried to answer her 'why' questions. Coping with such existential feelings of guilt and doubt can be an important growing point in the grief process. The development of courage to face these questions and feelings can lead us to live life more fully and to become more at one with our humanity and our own limitations.

Depression. Episodes of sadness are very understandable and natural following the death of someone close to you. It is like having a heavy weight placed on you, so that every task takes longer to perform and even the simplest things become a burden. This is often accompanied by a sense of futility and feelings of isolation. 'What's the point, who is going to see, why should I bother?'[5] These episodes are usually only transient and within the space of the same day one can move from sadness to a more normal mood. In contrast the depressed person, as opposed to the grief-stricken person, will be more persistently downcast and pessimistic, will not usually respond to warmth and reassurance, and will have a lasting sense of inner emptiness.

It is important not to apply the label 'depressed' to someone who is naturally sad. If someone has a tendency towards depressive illness then a major loss may reactivate an episode of endogenous depression – that is, a depression with an internal rather than external cause. Some people may develop a depressive illness as a reaction to the events surrounding the loss. Differentiating depression from sadness may require specialist help but, as a rule of thumb, sadness is usually more transient and the person's mood can lighten and change through sharing with others.

Usually when the bereaved person is feeling depressed he or she will withdraw from people because they will feel themselves to be unlovable and a leper: 'I taint people with death and I make them feel uncomfortable.' Feelings of low self-esteem may lead to harsh self-judgements, and those seeking to help need to be warm in their approach and positive. It is important to help the person towards a more objective and accurate balance sheet of their life. Death also produces a feeling of helplessness and impotence in that we feel unable to influence what happens to us. This can lead us to echo the words of Alexander Pope, 'Past hope, past cure, past help.' Fortunately such feelings do not last long but the bereaved person does want the feeling to be accepted for what it is and not to be told to 'snap out of it' or 'pull yourself together'. Although such episodes may recur frequently, listening with acceptance and genuine warmth and understanding goes a long way towards lifting the oppressive feelings of depression from the grief stricken. Prolongation of such episodes usually indicates the need for professional help.

The various feelings that have been described with reference to the Jenkins family, and others, tend to flow back and forth during the process of grief. To continue the analogy used earlier, it is rather like the tide coming in and out each day. Each time the tide comes up the beach you don't know what it will leave behind as it recedes. One day anger, another time depression, another outbursts of grief. Although analogies can mislead, this way of describing the process at least helps us to appreciate that over the course of time we experience a variety of feelings, not in a set order and sometimes recurring. Some of the feelings, as we have seen with the Jenkins family, can be very strong and may lead people to think in terms of sedation. This may occasionally be necessary medically, but we should always ask whether the decision about sedation is to enable the bereaved to cope or to help us to cope. Usually one finds that the use of sedation leads to the postponement of grief and not its resolution. Sedation by alcohol has a similar effect also!

Resolution

Eventually, the various conflicts and feelings are resolved and a new identity begins to be established. This takes many months and one usually thinks in terms of at least 18 months to two years before one expects to see any completion of mourning. The time-scale can be affected by many things. If the person is able, and has time, to commence their grieving before the death occurs then this will affect the process in that some of the reactions will have been worked through before the death occurs. However, when the actual death happens it does not mean that these feelings will not reoccur, but usually they will not be so forceful.

On the other hand, drowning your sorrows, as Mr Jenkins tried to do, merely prolongs grief in that you are avoiding it temporarily but it still remains to be faced. Mrs Jenkins was also trying to find a way to avoid working through her grief in that her new baby had to be a new Craig so that she could put the clock back and almost pretend it hadn't happened. With the vicar, Mrs Jenkins was putting him in the role of the nice, kind, understanding 'husband' who understood her better than her own husband. She retreated into fantasy and, quite rightly, the vicar recognized the need for professional help.

The process of resolution has several aspects:

1 To resolve that one *will* cope with the loss though it is not always easy to think of oneself as 'widowed' or 'childless'.

2 The frequent idealizing of the deceased, which often occurs earlier on.

3 The sense of detachment which comes from this idealization and which brings the ability to think and discuss the deceased realistically and comfortably.

4 A desire to relocate the deceased within their emotional life.[6] This means that the dead person will continue always to be part of one's life, but one will not be enslaved to the deceased.

5 A final resolution that one can enjoy oneself again and make new social contacts, without feeling disloyal to the deceased. Cultural factors are important here, as are organizations such as Cruse in helping the bereaved to accept a new status in society.

Table 1 summarizes many of the reactions that we have discussed and offers a tentative time-scale for normal bereavement behaviour.

The funeral *can* be a very important part of the grief process in that it can provide an opportunity and atmosphere for the expression of feelings that we may feel unable to express elsewhere. Within the context of the funeral the bereaved is removed from some of the constraints that may prevent the expression of grief. In some cultures there are official mourners and 'wailers' whose role is to initiate the expression of deep emotion. We shall return to a discussion of the place of the funeral in the grief process later (see Chapter 5).

The first anniversary can be especially painful for the bereaved, as can events such as Christmas and birthdays, which can thrust the person back into earlier grief reactions for a short period. This can happen even if, to all intents and purposes, the person has resolved their grief. Similarly a subsequent death or major loss can have the effect of re-awakening the previous grief.

Models and theories

Various models and theories have been developed which enable us to understand what is happening to people following a death. A model is primarily a descriptive way of categorizing the responses observed or experienced, whereas a theory seeks to offer an understanding of the causation of the various reactions. Recent years have seen a considerable growth in research interest in this area. In particular, researchers have sought to explore the impact of grief on medical and psychiatric problems, many of which pre-exist the bereavement. We shall discuss the relationship between grief and illness in Chapter 6 with reference to the research findings.

	DENIAL **Death of spouse** up to two weeks	DEVELOPING AWARENESS two weeks–two years	RESOLUTION two–five years or more
Physical reactions	Shock	Loss of vitality. Physical symptoms of stress. Irrational behaviour – often coming in waves lasting 20–60 mins. Psychosomatic illness, often parallels symptoms of deceased. (May not be reversed.)	
Emotional	Numbness Cotton-wool feeling	Outbursts of grief (pining, crying, exhaustion) Depression or sadness Anger – against deceased, medicine, God ('why') Loss of confidence and self-approval Guilt ('If only . . .') Loneliness – especially in older bereaved Idealizing of the deceased	'Resolution' 1 The resolve that one will cope 2 Sense of detachment allowing freedom of action 3 Emotional relocation of the deceased 4 Feeling it is now okay to enjoy social contacts, etc
External factors affecting behaviour	Circumstances of death and funeral arrangements Family Religious beliefs and culture	Financial loss or gain Loss of status Anniversaries Society's disapproval of overt emotion and avoidance of death	Acceptance of new status by society. Role of organizations such as Cruse and The Compassionate Friends

NB Grief work may commence prior to the death of the patient.

Table 1. 'Normal' patterns of bereavement behaviour

Before thinking about models and theories, it is important to distinguish terms frequently used in this area of care.

Bereavement   The objective situation or state of having lost someone significant.

Grief   The emotional response, feelings expressed following a loss and therefore highly individualized.

Mourning   The actions and way in which the grief is expressed. Often shaped and influenced by the practices of a culture or religious faith group.

Models

There are three models which should be considered briefly at this point: the phase model, the medical model and the grief work model.

In the *phase model* it is envisaged that the bereaved person moves over time through a series of phases, the number and description of which varies for different authors. Thus Elizabeth Kubler-Ross[7] talks of five stages, Bowlby[8] and Parkes[9] of four and others of eight. Such phases are to be seen as a classification of the reactions and not prescriptive of grief. Sadly people have tended to take Kubler-Ross's stages as sequential and steer people through them in the 'right' order. While grief is seen as a process in this model, people will move back and forth until they achieve some form of resolution.

The *medical model* sees all grief as pathological, or at the very least an illness which is painful and requires appropriate treatment. In some ways the concept of 'compassionate' leave seems to mirror this model in that in order to make proper arrangements for and attend a funeral (in the UK) extra time off work is required. This is usually provided for, via the family doctor, by being signed off sick.

The *grief work model* is based on Freud's work on mourning and melancholia, where it is acknowledged that we need time to test reality without the deceased around. We should not avoid doing this psychological work in the immediate aftermath, as well as later, for the sake of our future mental health.

Walter's *biographical model*[10] develops the idea that people benefit from talking to others about the deceased person and their life. This provides a way of the bereaved 'keeping hold' of the dead so that their memory is a continuous presence. This model encourages living with the past in order to gain strength to face the future. Stroebe[11] advocates, on the basis of her research, a *dual-process model* whereby the bereaved oscillate between confronting and avoiding reality.

Theories

Several theories have been developed to explain why people might react as they do and to help carers make appropriate and helpful interventions.

Crisis theory was developed especially by Caplan,[12] who said that in a crisis our equilibrium is disturbed. We seek to go back and recover our earlier equilibrium, until we realize we cannot achieve this but must use our previous coping strategies to achieve a new equilibrium. If previous coping ways don't help us we may need to develop new ones. Their process is accompanied by the characteristic reactions to danger. However, if the crisis is major (as in major disaster) this may lead to excess trauma and what is now known as post-traumatic stress disorder (PTSD) and classified as an illness. This theory is helpful, but in many ways too simplistic (see p. 62).

Psycho-analytic theory explains grief in terms of the way in which intolerable pain is repressed into the unconscious mind. From time to time it will surface to consciousness in a somewhat distorted and distressing way. Therapy can be especially effective for delayed or distorted grief patterns.

Learning theory sees unusual grief as a phobic avoidance of reality, rather than repression, and advocates 'flooding' to confront what is being avoided. This approach has been adopted in a modified form as a technique for helping people following a trauma. This helps some people but can be as traumatizing as the original experience.

John Bowlby developed the understanding of *attachment and separation* whereby the child experiences pangs of grief when separated from the mother. The severance of the bond or attachment between parent and child can be traumatic and can lead to 'clinging' behaviour which, if not coped with, leads in later life to a clinging to the dead. Parkes developed theories in terms of how we establish a new identity when realizing that the world we know is no longer the same as it used to be. Our previous (assumptive) world is different from the (real) world we now find ourselves in following our encounter with death. This leads to a process of transition (psycho-social transition) by which we reconstruct a new relationship with the deceased. This is echoed in Worden's fourth task of grief, which is to 'relocate' the dead so that they can be related to in a new way.

These different theories complement each other. Each contributes to our understanding of the similarities and differences between individual and group responses to bereavement. In particular they are supported by research evidence and have not been formed from anecdotal sources.

Grief is a very complex process and so it is not surprising, therefore, that for some it continues for a long time, or is never really completed, while for others it seems to progress gradually *without the need for any sort of intervention* except for a sensitive listening ear. If we are able to relate to the bereaved person and to be alongside them as a warm human being then perhaps we will be able to absorb the anger, together with the depressed and withdrawn periods. By accepting the other person with any ambivalent or negative feelings that they may have, we may thus be able to give the person the freedom to express grief in his or her own way, and so to use this experience of loss as an opportunity for growth.

Notes

1 C. S. Lewis, *A Grief Observed* (Faber, 1973), p. 7.
2 P. W. Speck, 'The Hospital Visitor', *Nursing Times* (5 July 1973).
3 P. Tillich, *The Courage to Be* (Fontana, 1979), p. 160.
4 ibid., p. 58.
5 C. S. Lewis, in *A Grief Observed*, describes this as the laziness of grief.
6 J. W. Worden, *Grief Counselling and Grief Therapy*, 2nd edn (Routledge, 1991).
7 E. Kubler-Ross, *On Death and Dying* (Routledge, 1990).
8 J. Bowlby, *Attachment and Loss, Vol. iii: Loss, sadness, and depression* (Penguin, 1981).
9 C. M. Parkes, *Bereavement: Studies of Grief in Adult Life*, 3rd edn (Penguin, 1996).
10 T. Walter, 'A New Model of Grief: Bereavement and Biography', *Mortality*, 1 (1996), pp. 7–25.
11 M. S. Stroebe, W. Stroebe and R. O. Hansson, *Handbook of*

Bereavement: Theory, Research and Intervention (Cambridge University Press, 1993).

12 G. Caplan, *An Approach to Community Mental Health* (Tavistock, 1961).

TWO

Opportunity for Growth – Facing our own Death

And how, if you were to die yourself? You know you must. Only be ready for it by the preparation of a good life, and then it is the greatest good that ever happened to thee.[1]

The prospect of personal death is an uncomfortable one for most people and is usually only contemplated when circumstances force us to do so. Our attitudes towards life, death and life after death will influence how we react to the realization that we may soon die. Equally important will be the manner in which death comes and our fear of pain, loss of dignity, and anxiety about those we leave behind. The extent to which we are able to cope with these anxieties will determine the extent to which we can agree with Jeremy Taylor in saying that death can be the 'greatest good that ever happened to thee'.

Colin and Anne were in their mid-thirties and had been married for 14 years. They had two children, John aged 13 years and Mary aged ten. Colin had a good job with a firm of architects and they had recently moved into a new house with a larger mortgage commitment. Anne was a nurse and had recently gone back to nursing part time. Colin had felt generally unwell for several weeks. Then he began to have a series of very heavy nosebleeds and over one weekend developed a great sense of weakness. By Monday he felt very ill and Anne called the doctor who referred Colin to the local hospital where the specialist admitted him to the ward for tests and blood transfusion.

Several days later, at the end of visiting time, Anne was seen by one of the doctors. He told her that the initial tests had been completed and that they believed Colin to have leukaemia. He said that, as a nurse, she would appreciate what that meant, but they wished to give Colin more blood and to put him onto drug therapy in the hope that they might induce a remission. He suggested that at this early stage, since mental attitude was important, they should only tell Colin that he had severe anaemia. Somewhat numbed and shocked Anne nodded and left the office. She found her way to the hospital chapel and sat there, crying, for a long time until she felt calm enough to make her way home. Anne's parents lived nearby and because of their close relationship with Anne and Colin were a great support to Anne in the months that followed the diagnosis of Colin's illness.

Colin made a good response to treatment and, since he was feeling so much better, seemed to accept that it was anaemia which was now under control. He did not ask anyone what had caused the anaemia. He was discharged home, resumed work, and made periodic visits to the out-patient clinic. Over the months that followed Colin was admitted to hospital several times for blood transfusions, but usually only stayed overnight. Because Colin worked as an architect he was able to work at home on the days when he felt unable to travel to the office and the spare bedroom was fitted out as a 'drawing office'.

When the initial shock had worn off, Anne decided to keep the knowledge of the diagnosis to herself and her parents. She looked to her parents for support as she sought to readjust to what she now knew. She read about leukaemia and prayed that all would be well. Anne found it hard to keep the knowledge from her husband and felt very deceitful. However, she also felt it was not yet the right time to share it with Colin and managed, for the most part, to shut it from her mind. About 18 months after diagnosis, Colin was taken ill again and readmitted into hospital. During the course of a ward round Colin overheard a medical student use the word 'leukaemia'. He felt cold inside and found that he could not think straight. Later he tried to convince himself that the student had been talking about someone else, but the nagging doubt remained.

Colin became very withdrawn and would not say why. The following night he slept badly and at about 1 a.m. a young student nurse offered him some cocoa. He told her very curtly that it was not cocoa that he wanted and she asked why he had suddenly become so restless. He said, 'I know I'm going to die, I heard the doctors say so.' Not quite sure what to say the nurse said, 'I think you must have misunderstood and I will get night sister to come and talk to you.' When the night sister arrived Colin was quiet for a while and then told her what he had overheard. He said that if it were true, then he wished to know all the facts about the illness and the treatment. The night sister then called the doctor who came and apologized for the way in which Colin had learnt his diagnosis and then Colin, the night sister and the doctor sat down and discussed the illness, treatment and the possibility of further remissions. At first Colin was very angry at the way in which he had been 'fooled' into believing it was anaemia, but he later admitted that he hadn't asked any questions about his illness because he was afraid to. The doctor let Colin express his anger with the hospital, with his wife and with himself for not questioning more. Colin thanked him for 'levelling with him' and then asked to be left alone.

The next morning Colin telephoned his wife and asked her to come to visit him as soon as the children had gone to school. When she arrived he told her what had happened the previous evening and then he cried for the first time. Later Colin became very practical and produced a lot of notes that he had written the night before, detailing what needed to be done about the mortgage, insurance policies, will and some of the jobs that he still had to finish for his firm. Although it was very stressful for them both they subsequently commented that they felt much more peaceful and calm after they had shared what each knew and feared. The conspiracy of silence was ended, Colin was now very tired and went off into a deep sleep.

Colin and Anne later asked for a second opinion and this was arranged. In fact Colin was seen by several consultants and the diagnosis of leukaemia was confirmed. His condition deteriorated over the next few weeks and he needed a great deal of reassurance from Anne that she and the family would cope if he died. He frequently said that he felt he had let her down in becoming ill and that he wished they could have longer. The children, who knew that Dad was seriously ill, became very helpful in and around the home – doing many of the things that he used to do to show that things were not falling apart without Dad. In some ways perhaps they coped too well, from Colin's point of view.

The hospital chaplain and Colin had formed a good relationship. During one of the chaplain's visits Colin expressed some of his anger and sense of unfairness that this should happen to him. 'I wish that I could see my children grow up and settle in life. I suppose you could not put in a good word upstairs, could you?' At times Colin would be very withdrawn and would not speak to anyone. At other times he would be writing off to travel agents for holiday brochures and making plans for a big family holiday. There were occasions when Colin would be very nasty with Anne (usually when the children were not visiting) and seemed to resent the fact that she was healthy. He would reduce her to tears and then be filled with remorse for the way he had behaved. On one such occasion Colin accused Anne of having an affair with someone else, said that she would be glad when he was dead so that she could have an active man again. After this latter outburst Anne left the ward hurriedly and went to the chapel in great distress where she was found by the chaplain. Gradually, after many tissues and some coffee, she explained what had happened and he was able to help her to see that Colin could only hit out at her. Because of their love for each other Colin felt it safe to vent his wrath on Anne. If he hit out at the nurses or doctors they might tell him 'to get on with it alone'. Then Anne and the chaplain talked about some of the fears and anxieties that Colin had. He was finding it almost intolerable to face 'letting go' of wife, family and life itself. He was afraid of dying (though not of death) and feared dying in pain or losing his dignity. The drugs he had received had already led to the loss of his hair, although it was now growing again. There had been times when Anne had found Colin withdrawn and she had felt rejected – especially when she found he was talking to the chaplain about certain feelings and reactions and not to her!

As a result of this discussion Anne was able to accept that Colin needed someone from outside the family to whom he could talk confidentially. The next day the chaplain visited while Anne and Colin were together. He asked Colin, 'How did you both meet?' Then as they talked about their first meeting he gradually led them to talk about their courtship, marriage, birth of the children. Bit by bit they were being put in touch once again with their earlier life together and, amid much laughter, remembering many of the funny things that had happened to them. When they reached the time of Colin's illness Colin was quiet for a while and then said, 'We've had a very good life, haven't we?'

Colin and Anne were both communicant members of the Church of England and Colin asked about anointing and healing. Following discussion it was arranged that the chaplain should bring them both Communion later in the day and that they should be anointed. The chaplain spoke to their parish priest, who had kept in touch with Colin and Anne, and he arranged to come to the ward and take part in the service. The children and the ward sister also joined them for the service, after which Colin and Anne remarked on the sense of peace which they both felt. In the days that followed everyone seemed to be as prepared as they could be for Colin's death, while still enjoying the life that he had left.

Then Colin went into remission and the medical staff were talking about him 'going home'! The reactions in all concerned were a mixture of pleasure, joy, apprehension and disbelief. Two days after his discharge the chaplain received a telephone call from Colin. 'It's a weird feeling,' he said, 'I feel that I am having to be born into my own family all over again. It's as if I have come back from the dead.' It took quite a while for the family to readjust to being a 'Mum, Dad and two children' again, and Anne's parents and the local vicar were very important in helping them to settle down. The family had been facing up to the implications of Colin's diagnosis for so long that they had worked through a lot of their grief and so were almost waiting for his death – which had not happened. They were left with a strange feeling of guilt and resentment and pleasure that he was still with them. At the back of their minds was the anxiety that sooner or later they might have to face this all over again. A few months later there was another telephone call from Colin to say that things were 100 per cent better and that, if anything, the whole experience had led Colin and Anne to fall in love all over again.

A year later Colin had to be readmitted to hospital where he failed to respond to treatment. Colin slept a great deal and did not say very much. Anne and her mother were sitting with him when he died, very peacefully and calmly. Although the family were thrown back into their grief there was a real feeling that they had grown during the previous two years and that Colin's death could not be described as a failure. They had learnt to 'let go' and to grow on. As Anne was later able to say, 'It sounds odd perhaps, but through Colin's illness and death I feel that we have all grown - including Colin!'

The reactions of Colin are similar to those experienced by many people when they realize that they must face the fact of personal death. His reactions also parallel those already described in relation to the bereaved following a death, the difference being that the dying person is grieving for the *impending loss* of his or her own life. The grief reaction of the family also frequently commences before the death occurs and thus provides another reason for the parallel reactions of Shock and disbelief; Growing awareness; Resolution.

Shock and disbelief

The bereaved frequently experience shock following the death, and for the dying person the knowledge that one might soon die precipitates a crisis with accompanying feelings of shock, panic and an inability to believe it. This was certainly the case for Colin, who tried to convince himself that the medical student was talking about someone else when he used the word 'leukaemia'. The extent to which we deny the knowledge is often related to our preparedness to receive the news and the way in which it is imparted to us.

A dying person receives communications from many people and on occasions these messages may be confused and ambiguous, thus creating anxiety. Other communications may match the thoughts and feelings of the patient and help the person to make sense of what is being experienced. Some of the ways in which we receive information include:

1 Direct statements from doctor, nurse or other person.
2 Overheard comments made by staff, family or others.
3 Changes in treatment, position of bed in ward, etc.
4 Changes in behaviour observed in other people.
5 Self-diagnosis - reading medical dictionaries!
6 Alteration of symptoms, especially if they do not fit in with what you have already been told or led to expect.
7 An alteration in the attitude of others towards your future plans or job prospects.

The dying person will sometimes say, when the shock has

worn off, that they knew deep down that 'things were not good'. Although they may have denied their diagnosis to themselves and to others the above sources of information have often conveyed the seriousness of their condition. This may be borne out by such comments as: 'It was their eyes that told me. They smiled with their mouths, but their eyes were sad'; or 'After the results came back the doctors didn't stay long with me, or would avoid me. I felt written off.' Colin requested all the information he could get about his condition, partly so that he knew what he had to face and partly so that he could confirm his worst fears. He was fortunate in having medical and nursing staff who would recognize his need and respond with an honest sharing of information. Sometimes our own anxieties about death and dying block any real sharing and lead instead to evasion and avoidance.

It is clear, therefore, that whatever *we* may decide about sharing what we know concerning the patient's prognosis the dying person will have already received a lot of communication from those around them and made various deductions of their own. Anyone who has gone through a range of tests, investigations, operations and subsequent treatment will have reached some conclusion, even if this has not been discussed with others. It is only as we build up a relationship of trust and confidence that the sick person will feel that perhaps it is safe to share some of their feelings and fears.

If such a relationship has been formed it is often more a matter of letting oneself be told than actually telling the other person what is happening to them. For the minister a question such as 'What has the doctor or hospital been able to tell you?' will be fairly open-ended. It allows the sick person to reveal what they know or suspect but also gives them the opportunity to terminate this line of approach with a brief 'Nothing much, you know what hospitals are.'

There should be no set rules about what people are, or are not, told. Getting close enough to the dying person is the only way to resolve this question because the sort of information we may be giving (or withholding) is best shared in a loving, caring relationship. There also needs to be lateral consultation with others who are providing care.

It is important not to tell lies to patients, but this does not imply telling the whole truth all at once. The prognosis or outlook may change, the understanding of the 'truth' may alter, and so one should gradually reveal more as you know it and the patient indicates that they wish to receive it. Certainly, where the patient is asking 'How long have I got?' we should avoid specific answers. It is often better to say 'months rather than years' than to give a rigid 'two months'. A rigid and definitive time can have the effect of extinguishing hope, and we should beware of removing hope.

The answer to the question 'To tell or not to tell' lies more in our preparedness to get close to those who are dying, finding out what *they* wish to know, and then having the courage to share the reality with them.

Because the dying, not surprisingly, find it hard to believe that they may not recover from their illness, they will frequently seek several 'other opinions' in the hope that another hospital, doctor or treatment centre may be able to offer a better prognosis or cure. Sometimes this will lead to visits to healing centres where the sick person or their family may seek a miracle. So often physical healing may not occur but there may be a real healing of attitude and approach to the illness. Not all visits to healing centres are an expression of disbelief of a diagnosis, but this possibility should be borne in mind when discussing such centres with terminally ill people. Ministers may also need to remember that this may apply to the person's expectations of the sacraments as well.

Growing awareness

When the initial shock wears off the dying person enters a longer period of readjustment while maintaining a definite interest in life. With the awareness of his condition, Colin begins to express various emotions: anger, tears, remorse and a sense of urgency about getting the practical tasks completed as an expression of his anxiety for Anne and the children. We have already discussed many of these feelings in relation to the bereaved.

One new factor is Colin's attempt, through the chaplain, to *bargain* with God for more time. This has been described by Elizabeth Kubler-Ross[2] as one 'stage' in the reactions of dying people which may be revealed to clergy more often than to other people. This is because the dying person may see the minister as a confidential person who will not laugh at their request and their attempt to gain extra time. But the minister is also seen as someone who may be able to persuade God to agree to the request, 'I suppose you couldn't put in a good word upstairs ... ?' often said as a half joke.

Such bargaining is really an attempt to postpone the 'evil

hour' and may be linked with feelings of guilt for not having attended church more frequently or given more to charity. Quite often the person will make some promise of a gift of money if they can live until their son or daughter has been married. If you feel ill prepared to meet God face to face then it is not surprising that you should try to postpone the moment. A sensitive approach on the part of the clergyman may uncover some of the underlying guilt feelings and help the person to accept that, while bargaining is understandable, it is not a very helpful way of coping in the long term.

The dying have many anxieties and fears to cope with and it is only as one relates sensitively to the dying person that one may learn what these are. Some of these anxieties can be alleviated quite easily, others may prove very difficult.

Fear of the unknown and the importance of hope

In the very early stages of the realization of the nature of his illness Colin wanted information. This information was partly medical, partly nursing, in that he wanted to know about the disease, the treatment and to receive reassurance about the care he would receive in the future and whether he would die in pain. He wanted to know what lay ahead and what the *act* of dying would be like. During this early part of his grieving he was trying to sort out who he could trust with his questions, who would be honest in their answers and who would be honest enough to say, 'I do not know.' If he was going to die, then he was going to do it well!

There were several discussions with the chaplain and with other people concerning death, life after death and the nature of God. Colin was a practising Christian and felt guilty at questioning his beliefs. Nevertheless, he felt that he had to ask himself whether he really believed or was his faith only an intellectual acceptance of a belief system. He felt angry with God but also wondered if his own weak faith had contributed to his being ill. He needed to feel that it was all right to question God and to be angry with him. This is, of course, a feeling that is common to many dying people. Colin found much comfort from reading the Easter narratives and especially the references to Thomas with his doubts and uncertainties and the fact that Thomas was not rejected because he doubted. Tillich's phrase '. . . the courage to accept oneself as accepted in spite of being unacceptable'[3] was to be a key phrase at various points in his illness, because it held out to him the *hope* of being accepted even though at times he felt very unacceptable to God, himself and to his family.

Hope is an essential part of living as well as dying for it is a part of being. Hope involves us in remaining open to what may seem improbable possibilities. For Colin and Anne, apart from the Christian hope of a life after death, there had to be the hope concerning life at present which they expressed in terms of planning a family holiday. They both knew that the holiday would probably not come about, but the main pleasure seemed to be in the planning and the sharing of dreams and fantasy. No firm bookings were made and no money was paid since 'there would always be time to sort that out later'. Although you know that your life expectancy is short, you cannot make that the sole topic of conversation all the time.

Loss of family, friends, self-identity and one's body

Colin was naturally very anxious about his family and how they would cope without him. Together with Anne he tried to sort out the practical issues and, in some ways, seeing that she would cope was both a source of resentment as well as a comfort. Much of the anger that Colin expressed towards his wife stemmed from a resentment that she was well and he was not. He felt angry that his own body had become diseased and had let him down. When illness alters our appearance or our ability to perform the tasks we are used to doing we may experience a loss of self-esteem and self-integrity. Some people may ask for no visitors or a restriction of visitors if they feel this very keenly. A young woman who was dying with a very disfiguring cancer of the jaw felt that her body was visibly disintegrating and was rejecting her. At one point in her illness she asked for no visitors apart from her mother, her husband and the minister who was visiting her because she did not feel that she could cope with other people's reactions to what the disease was doing to her appearance. It was the loving contact with her family and others which helped this young woman to re-establish her self-esteem and to face people again. It was their loving touch which put her in contact with her own body once again and this underlines for us the importance of touch in the process of healing and re-establishment of identity.

Human contact affirms who we are and the dying person needs contact with his or her own self and others right to the last, so that he or she may remain a person and so not be reduced to a number or a case. The process of dying will sometimes awaken submerged feelings of dislike or hatred, as well as feelings of love and tenderness, towards family members and others. It is important to help the dying and their family and friends to understand and accept the variety of sometimes conflicting emotions that may arise. The way in which drugs are used will have an effect on how the dying are able to sort out these feelings. In some cultures people will refuse any medication which will cloud their thought because they wish to approach death with a clear mind. In the case of the Buddhist, for example, a person's next life through reincarnation is dependent upon the quality of their present life and they will not want to spoil it in their last hours. The same can be said for many non-Buddhists.

It is when the dying have been able to reaffirm the nature and value of some of their relationships that they can then achieve a measure of peace which can help them to separate from their loved ones. Another factor which helps them in the separation is a belief in the after-life because it reaffirms the continuity of one's being, and the belief that we will be reunited with those who have already died. In this way, the dying may find comfort in the knowledge that the present separation, painful though it is, is only a temporary one.

The fear of loneliness, pain and suffering

Closely associated with the loss of identity and of one's body is the fear of pain and isolation. If you are ill in bed with a non-fatal illness, such as flu, you can feel very isolated in the upstairs bedroom while the family are continuing everyday life downstairs. It can be very tempting to keep banging on the floor in order to be reassured that you have not been forgotten. If you are ill in hospital this feeling can be heightened, especially at visiting times if your visitors are late or are not coming. At one point in his illness Colin accuses his wife of adultery because she always looked 'happy' when visiting and, in his fantasy, she must already be getting used to life without him by having a lover.

In seeking to prevent loneliness one needs to be aware of the danger of never allowing the dying time to be alone! It is a matter of reassuring the dying person that people are available to the extent that he or she needs and desires them to be. In conversing with the dying person it is helpful if we remember not to make their dying the sole focus, but to spend time engaging the person in everyday tasks and interests as far as they wish. In their better moments, the dying need to be able to re-enter the family if we are to avoid the extreme situation that Colin experienced where he had 'died' socially before he died physically.

Many people associate dying with pain and suffering and pray for a 'good, peaceful end'. Pain is an important factor in creating loneliness and isolation. If pain seems to have some purpose or meaning (e.g. the pain experienced following an operation while the wound heals) then we can usually bear it more easily, or at least put up with it. If however the pain is needless or seemingly unnecessary it becomes suffering and cannot usually be borne for long. 'Man is not destroyed by suffering, he is destroyed by suffering without meaning.'[4] The minister of religion may be seen as someone who comes to encourage stoicism and martyrdom. Being involved with life and other people is also an important factor in coping with pain. The control of pain is something requiring a variety of approaches including medication, involvement of other people, information about the causes of the pain, and the involvement of the patients in their own management of pain. Pain and the anticipation of it can very quickly demoralize and is a very important aspect of terminal care, as the Hospice movement has been able to show. It is important that clergy endeavour to liaise with the Macmillan service or equivalent home care team within the health district.

Loss of dignity and self-control

Many dying people are afraid that as their illness progresses they will lose control over various bodily functions and therefore also lose some of their dignity. Colin had already suffered hair loss as a result of the drugs he had received and he found it hard to accept that he might become even weaker and more dependent upon others. The loss of independence and control of your body or mind can be a frightening prospect. Although there may be times when it is nice to be allowed to regress and be cared for, after a while it can become very irritating and smothering. If relatives find it satisfying to have 'someone to care for' it can be difficult for them to encourage the sick person towards whatever degree of independence is possible, and to allow them to make their own decisions about what happens to themselves.

From the beginning Colin made it clear that he wished to

maintain a strong measure of control over what was told to him as well as what would happen to his family through the provision of a will and the checking of insurance cover, etc. The relinquishing of responsibility should be a gradual process for most people. In Colin's and Anne's case it happened a bit too quickly in that he handed 'everything' over and then failed to die! This could not be foreseen at the time but the feeling of having to be reborn into his family might not have been so acute had Colin retained a greater measure of control for longer. Against this one must say that had Colin died instead of going into remission we might have concluded that it was a 'perfect' resolution with everybody ready and the patient dying on time!

An important prayer for Colin at various times was the prayer for serenity, 'Lord, grant me the serenity to accept the things I cannot change, the courage to change the things I can, and the wisdom to know the difference' (Reinhold Niebuhr).

Decision-making and patient choice

Colin was concerned to maintain control for as long as possible. Since the time of his death there have been many changes in the ways in which people can maintain an involvement in decision-making in a variety of clinical situations. Exercising these choices can be very influential in the way in which people face the prospect of their own death.

Advance directives or 'living wills'

These are formal statements of the personal values, views and preferences regarding treatment or non-treatment in the event of specific events happening to the individual. These statements are drawn up in advance and may nominate a proxy to act in one's place when mental incapacity or inability to communicate make participation in decision-making difficult or impossible. Such directives are helpful to medical staff and are now usually taken into account, though some are framed too generally to be helpful. They also need to be reviewed and revised frequently since circumstances and views may change with time. Requests for illegal procedures cannot be complied with, though what is possible and permissible in the UK changes as a result of various decisions in the High Court.

Consent and treatment decisions

Giving or withholding consent with regard to treatment depends upon adequate information, competence to make a decision and a lack of coercion or pressure. It is when the patient is deemed incompetent that most difficulties arise of an ethical nature, e.g. whether or not to start antibiotics in a patient on life-support or whether to withhold food or fluids in a patient who has gone into a coma which appears irreversible. Deciding what the patient would want if able to say so can be difficult. Withholding and withdrawing treatment are often described as *omissions* and *acts*. The question often is, what would be obligatory treatment and what would be extraordinary. Clear guidelines have come from the High Courts and the BMA in respect of patients in what has been described as 'persistent vegetative state' or with 'brain stem death'. In other cases carers have to exercise clinical judgements and balance the risk-benefit with an assessment of quality of life. Here again an advance directive can be helpful.

Physician-assisted suicide

The fear of the dying process can lead some people to seek to end their life before its natural conclusion. If they are physically unable to achieve this for themselves, as in the case of people with advanced motor neurone disease, Huntington's Chorea or AIDS, then they may seek the help of someone else. It is a criminal offence in the UK at present actively to assist someone else to die. This applies even if one supplies the information and/or the means but is not present at the time. Compassion and emotional involvement can lead people to agree to various forms of help, as testified in court cases in the UK and elsewhere. A distinction must be made between actively removing another's life as the prime intention and a person dying as a secondary effect of a treatment or drug primarily designed to alleviate suffering or pain. This is often described as the principle of double effect, whereby the act is primarily intended to have a good effect, e.g. diamorphine to alleviate pain, but may secondarily depress breathing and shorten the life.

Resuscitation

The prospect of being resuscitated may either be comforting or alarming. One of the main anxieties relates to possible outcome. If one can be sure of a good outcome, the resuscitation would be welcomed and expected. However, views may vary if the outlook could be permanent damage or death following a long stay in an intensive care unit. The usual problems necessitating resuscitation concern the airway, breathing and circulation (often referred to as the ABC of life-support). Restoring function in any of these will be straightforward in most cases. However, in some circumstances an advance directive may state clearly that no resuscitation should be attempted, or a known malignant disease may indicate that it would be harmful to resuscitate. It is good practice for hospitals to have an established policy giving clear guidelines to staff regarding the recording of resuscitation status and how that status has been established. If no information is available then one should presume in favour of the patient and review the case in the light of more information *after* resuscitation. Failure to resuscitate may lead to the death of somebody who is otherwise healthy and with continued life-support could be considered as a potential donor of organs for transplantation. We shall discuss this further in Chapter 5 (see p. 85).

These issues, of an ethical nature, can lead to conflict within the patient's family, in that various relatives may have different views on what is acceptable. If the patient is aware of this, these tensions may affect the way in which the patient approaches the end of their life and the achievement of any degree of inner peace and calm. Pastorally there may be a need for a ministry of reconciliation to assist those involved to achieve some harmony. This may not always be possible and just as the dying frequently die the way they have lived, so the family will not necessarily change its mode of coping in the face of death.

Resolution – the approach of death

When talking about the reactions of bereaved people, we described how eventually many of the tensions and conflicts within them are resolved. The same is true for the dying person if he or she has sufficient time and support to cope with these feelings before the moment of death.

One of the most noticeable features of the final phase of dying is the way in which the person gradually withdraws from other people and appears depressed. When one considers the variety of losses experienced by the dying person, prior to the final loss of their own life, it is very natural and not surprising that they should have periods of depression. The depression seems to take two forms.

The first type of depression is that which clearly arises as a result of losses already experienced. It is akin to *reactive depression* and will respond very well to reassurance and encouragement. Sometimes drug therapy may be necessary, especially if the experience of loss has had the effect of triggering off any underlying mental illness.

Towards the end of the person's life one often sees a second type of depression which is not the result of past loss but is linked to impending loss. Here one sees depression being used as a tool to prepare for loss and to facilitate acceptance and the final letting go. Sadness may be a better term to use. If *our* anxiety causes us to encourage the dying person to look on the bright side and does not allow them to be sad, then our reassurances will be meaningless and we shall have made it clear that we cannot share this part of the experience with them. On the other hand, if we are able to permit the dying to express sorrow, to be sad, quiet or withdrawn then we shall have done much to ease the isolation of this final phase. 'You didn't say much, but you let me be sad. Thank you.'

This part of dying is marked by its silences, when communication is more non-verbal than verbal, where much more is conveyed by the touch of the hand and a silent sitting together. Too much interruption and interference by relatives and others in an attempt to 'cheer up' the patient will often irritate because it cuts across the person's emotional and spiritual preparation. It is usual for the dying to sleep a great deal at this latter phase and the minister may find when visiting that the person may open his or her eyes, smile, hold the minister's hand, perhaps ask for a prayer or blessing and then drift back into sleep. This, of course, assumes that there has been a good relationship between the dying person and the minister prior to this visit. If the person has an ambivalent feeling about clergy, or reacts to a stereotype image, then to open the eyes and see a minister may have an alarming rather than comforting effect. Although this situation can be dealt with if it happens it is a great help if the minister has been given the opportunity to relate with the dying person long before the terminal stage. Where there has been a long and meaningful relationship the visit of the minister with an appropriate prayer and blessing can bring the release that the person seemed to be waiting for.

An 18-year-old girl who was suffering from leukaemia was

readmitted to hospital. Her parish priest, who knew her well, visited her in hospital and, together with the hospital chaplain, anointed her. Over the next few weeks her condition deteriorated and she was visited regularly by the parish priest and hospital chaplain. One evening the chaplain was sitting with her, neither saying very much. As he got up to leave he said that he would see her the next day and, placing his hands on her head, said a short prayer of commendation and blessed her. He turned to leave and as he did so she said, 'Wait'. Then she said 'Goodbye', gave a deep sigh, and died. He felt sure at that time that the prayer, commendation and blessing had led her to feel that now was the time to 'let go'. Such a 'perfect end' is rare and quite often the death occurs when you have just left the person in order to get a cup of tea or post a letter. One should beware of feeling guilty about this and burdening oneself with 'If only . . .'

The above discussion of the process of dying is derived from the experience of Colin as well as that of other people. However, these reactions, of both the dying and the bereaved, are modified greatly by the circumstances surrounding the death as well as the personalities of the people involved. It is important that the dying should be allowed to die their own death rather than be forced to fit the pattern of behaviour imposed by the hospital, institution or by the expectations of family or society.[5] One of the dangers inherent in trying to describe the process of dying is that people then take the described pattern as the norm and attempt to fit people to it. In so doing we are failing to respond to the dying or the bereaved *where they are*; instead we are reacting to them at the point we feel they should have reached. The problem is that the dying person may not have read the book! We are in the same situation as the mother who becomes worried that her child does not conform to the pattern described in her baby book – the baby has not read the book either. Mother and baby normally, of course, teach each other.

One person who has contributed greatly to our understanding of the reactions of a dying person is Dr Elizabeth Kubler-Ross, who interviewed over two hundred terminally ill patients. As a result of these interviews she proposed a model to help us to understand what she described as the various *stages* in coming to terms with our own death: Denial and Isolation, Anger, Bargaining, Depression, Acceptance and Hope.[6]

In describing these different stages Dr Kubler-Ross gives

many examples of people who do not follow this sequential process, but it is a very convenient way of classifying what people may be experiencing. Because of this, unfortunately, some people have referred to these stages as a normal sequence of events and inferred that any deviation from this pattern is abnormal. Such does not seem to have been Dr Kubler-Ross's intention. What she was offering was a useful way of identifying people's feelings without dictating a set order. She was not offering people a framework within which the person was allowed to die!

In her autobiography of her own dying experience JoAnn Smith describes her confusion when she realized that she was not following the 'prescribed pattern'. After struggling with this she concludes: 'The stages of dying are not necessarily chronological. In my own experience I have moved back and forth through several of these a number of times.'[7]

Schulz and Aderman[8] conclude that each patient will 'adopt a pattern of behaviour' which persists until death occurs. There may be a lot of similarity in the reactions of different people, however, and there also seems to be much flowing back and forth of these feelings. An analogy that has helped some people is that of the tide. Beachcombers are well aware of the way in which the character of the beach can change with each tide. One day the tide deposits driftwood and seaweed. Another day it deposits dead seabirds, oil or sewage. After another tidal flow the beach may be swept clean of all debris. One cannot be sure from day to day what you will find on the beach. The same would seem to be true of grief. This analogy of the tide flowing back and forth and depositing anger or tears or sadness or cheerfulness seems to reflect the comment made by many people, 'All of a sudden I just became angry, it swept over me.'

In relating with the dying and the bereaved it would seem our task is to be sensitive and try to identify the particular stresses that they are experiencing *at that moment*. Then we should try to respond to the emotions and needs expressed – this will often mean offering practical help (getting the district nurse, doctor, a commode, a night-sitter), or offering emotional support (a box of tissues, a listening ear), or spiritual support (through the ministry of the word and sacraments as seems appropriate). In this way we shall not be imposing upon the dying or the bereaved *our* expectation of how they should react. Rather, we shall be reacting sensitively to how the person is *actually* feeling. Thus we allow the person to die their own death or to grieve their own grief and in this way we make easier the letting go.

Figure 1 illustrates three views of the world as a person may experience it during illness and while facing death, whether at home or in hospital. It is set out in a simplified way with many details omitted so that it can be read more clearly. The figure should not be taken as an exact description of what every terminally ill person experiences. It is essentially a framework which those who are involved with a dying person can use in an attempt to heighten their own understanding of what is happening.[9]

Near death experiences

This term was first coined by Dr Raymond Moody in 1975, when he described the experiences of people who claimed to have had a near death experience (NDE) following a traumatic life-threatening event. Moody identified 15 common elements in NDEs, including hearing news about oneself, feelings of peace and quiet, noise and/or music, the dark tunnel, being out of one's body, meeting others, the presence of light, coming back, telling others, new views of death, and feeling changed.

Subsequent work has shown that it is rare that two experiences are the same or that they cover all 15 of Moody's elements. Overall, however, people find it a pleasant experience which becomes more so as the experience continues. Occasionally NDEs can be frightening, especially if suicide or attempted murder features in the 'death event'.

Corroboration is difficult, although sometimes people can describe conversations or events which they would not be expected to have known or been party to. Some researchers claim that NDEs are accompanied by physiological and neurological changes. Whatever the mechanism involved, what is noticeable is the marked change in attitude which people undergo as a result of these experiences. People's views about death frequently change, with a reduction in the degree of fear and a frequent increase in spiritual awareness. This spiritual component is usually expressed through the cultural/ religious norms of the group to which the person belongs. Thus a Christian may subsequently describe meeting Jesus, a Muslim meeting Mohammed, or a Buddhist talking with Buddha.[10] The most impressive feature of NDEs is the impact they have on the belief and attitudes of those experiencing them.[11]

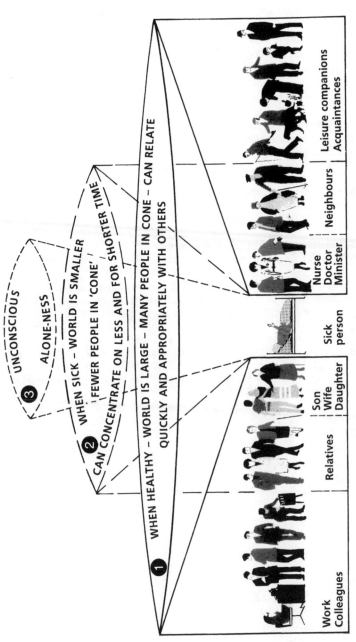

1. WHEN HEALTHY – WORLD IS LARGE – MANY PEOPLE IN CONE – CAN RELATE QUICKLY AND APPROPRIATELY WITH OTHERS

2. WHEN SICK – WORLD IS SMALLER – FEWER PEOPLE IN 'CONE' – CAN CONCENTRATE ON LESS AND FOR SHORTER TIME

3. UNCONSCIOUS – ALONE-NESS

Work Colleagues | Relatives | Son Wife Daughter | Sick person | Nurse Doctor Minister | Neighbours | Leisure companions Acquaintances

Figure 1. 'Cones of awareness': How the dying person's view of the world may change

Whatever the mechanism for these phenomena, they do seem to reflect other categories of religious experience. The potential to demonstrate that we can maintain an existence *outside* of our physical body could have profound implications for the belief in survival after death.

Notes

1 Jeremy Taylor, *Holy Living, Holy Dying* (Rivingtons, 1882).
2 E. Kubler-Ross, *On Death and Dying* (Routledge, 1990).
3 P. Tillich, *The Courage to Be* (Fontana, 1979), p. 160.
4 Viktor Frankl, *Man's Search for Meaning* (Hodder and Stoughton, 1963).
5 Requests for euthanasia often reflect the feeling that one is not receiving the care that he or she desires. See *On Dying Well* (Church Information Office, 1975).
6 Kubler-Ross, op. cit.
7 JoAnn Kelly Smith, *Free Fall* (SPCK, 1977), p. 48.
8 R. Schulz and D. Aderman, 'Clinical Research and the Stages of Dying', *Omega*, 5 (1974), pp. 137–43.
9 I am very grateful to the Revd Allan Reed, who was Chaplain of Massachusetts General Hospital, Boston, Mass., USA, while I was a Clinical Pastoral Education student there in 1970/71. He first set me thinking about the ideas which have developed into this figure and Figure 2 in Chapter 4. (I.A-S.)
10 P. Badham, 'Religious and near death experiences in relation to belief in a future life'. *Mortality*, 2:1 (1997) p. 10.
11 A. J. Ayer, 'What I saw when I died'. In P. Edwards, *Immortality* (Macmillan, 1992).

THREE

Letting Go

Dragons live for ever, but not so little boys.
(Last verse of song *Puff the Magic Dragon*)

'Pooh! . . . I'm not going to do Nothing any more.'
'Never again?'
'Well, not so much. They don't let you.'[1]

A television film on facing death and bereavement contained an important sequence which did not involve a funeral or even interviewing a group of newly bereaved people. An 18-month-old child was filmed playing in the sandpit with her mother in the park where they went together nearly every day. On this occasion her mother played with her for a time and then, while the child's attention was engrossed, left her and walked out of sight. The child subsequently played on, quite unconcerned, until the moment two or three minutes later when she realized that her mother had left her. At first she did not seem particularly concerned. Presumably she had coped with similar separations before, but when her mother failed to reappear the child ceased playing altogether and commenced a search for her mother which became increasingly desperate. She looked all around her and anxiously scanned the faces of other mothers with their children. Eventually she sat alone in the middle of the sandpit and sobbed uncontrollably. She stopped playing and resisted vigorously the attempts of any other adults or children to comfort her. She rocked to and fro and seemed completely absorbed in herself. Slowly, however, she began to play again, alone; and after a while she started playing, although fairly tentatively, with other children.

To a casual observer it looked as though the child was playing in exactly the same way as before her mother left, but this was not so. An experienced nursery nurse and mother, on being shown the film, immediately pointed out the differences in the little girl's way of playing, before and after her separation from her mother. When the child's mother reappeared the little girl ran up to her and hugged her and the reunion was complete. She could, of course, have behaved in other ways, possibly ignoring her mother, apparently punishing her for daring to abandon her. Although unable to express in words how she felt, the child's separation from her mother was the end of her world as she knew it. Her actions and feelings were in fact those which are typically seen in grieving people, children or adults. Much will depend of course on the nature of the loss, the age of the person, and whether the feelings are expressed in actions or words. Freud,[2] interestingly, points out that, to an external observer, bereaved people frequently behave identically to people who in another setting might be labelled 'mad'. Grief, which is not madness but part of the fear which surrounds the process of 'letting go', has to do with the confusion which is so often made between natural and important feelings connected with loss and what are sometimes taken as the manifestations of mental illness.

It is impossible to go far into the story of our individual growth and development without facing the key issues of letting go and being let go. At birth the infant is let go from the mother's womb to face a new world, one which is very different and which may feel hostile and strange. Its existence prior to birth has been mainly safe and secure and mother and child are physically one. Both may feel intensely the experience of separation which takes place at birth and which is, of course, crucial if each is to be a separate person, although tied together by genes and a very complex set of emotions. If you are capable of being attached to someone you have also to face the risk and pain of letting go. At birth the baby moves from one existence to the other and if the time and place are right for the child and for its mother he or she will be let go into the loving and caring hands of the doctor or midwife.

But letting go is a double-edged expression. It can imply being drawn gently into a new sort of existence; or being released or dragged into a void where nothing is safe and nothing consistent. At every point of life which involves growth there seems to be a need to look and feel backwards as well as forwards as an essential ingredient in managing the change successfully. Notions which adults take for granted, such as trust, do not come automatically to a young child, or a person facing a crisis like death, whether their own or that of someone close. When babies are left alone they are incapable of trusting their mother or father to come back to them. Bowlby and others argue that only after babies have some experience of being left and found again have they some framework against which to judge the world and begin to trust it.[5] (The simple game of Peep-Bo, much enjoyed by adults and babies, is in essence about losing and refinding, albeit in play.) These losses are necessary for the emotional growth of the infant.

It is precisely those feelings about whether it is possible to trust or not, and whether the world is a safe place or not, which we all of us meet in facing death and loss. The loss of a person, of a place, a stage in one's life or even the possible loss of one's self through one's own death, raise the possibility yet again of how safe it is to trust. Frequently people who are facing their own death, or the loss of a close friend or relation, will describe how their trust in themselves and in people close to them, and even in God, has been profoundly shaken by what has happened. The experience of loss is rather like losing the 'map' of our world which we have built up throughout our lives, and after every change it has to be built again but differently. This is not something which most of us manage by thinking about it. It seems to stem from our early experience of loss and how we have coped with it.

Many adults can describe vividly their first day at school, memories of which usually involve the loss of home and so many things connected with early childhood, rather than the benefits subsequently discovered! Altruism or a conscious encouragement of the child to think on the bright side and on the benefits which they are about to achieve have a limited value. It is very difficult to reassure any child or adult who does not feel some basic assurance on the basis of earlier losses and separations which have been painful but eventually tolerable. In the case of going to school, the separation involves both the child and the parents. There may be some mutual reluctance to let go and to be let go. (A teacher once commented to one of the authors that there was rarely a homesick child without a childsick parent!) It has been the experience of hospital staff that many people describe their admission to hospital as very similar to their first day at school.

A child who has a younger brother or sister born into the family, however well prepared for the event, will never have exactly the same position in the family again. The child will have had to abandon the position of youngest child in the family, a position with both benefits and disadvantages. One way of coping with the future may be to behave like the child he or she used to be. This process is sometimes called 'regression', going back in feelings and behaviour, to a way of coping which belongs to an earlier stage of life, when the outside world feels intolerable. It is one very important way of coping with loss which we shall encounter again.

The way in which attachments are built up during our life and especially during our early years turns out to be crucial as to how we cope with subsequent losses. 'Attachment theory' helps explain the 'bricks' that build up to develop a fuller way of coping with loss and change. It also helps us understand the significance of what are sometimes called psycho-social transitions. These are losses which may be significant but do not necessarily involve a physical death. One study examined which types of loss were most significant for the first three years after the event and suggested that divorce and separation carry a higher risk of psychiatric and psychological problems than the death of a partner! This may be highlighted by a sense of failure, real or imagined, together with feelings of guilt and responsibility.

One person who had been through a divorce commented to the hospital chaplain that she had no structure with which to take leave of a relationship which had been impossible prior to her divorce but which also represented 18 years of her life. The loss of a relationship can also involve the tragedy of facing lost potential. Pastoral care has, we believe, to walk a very careful path. The outside world tends to minimize losses like divorce and occasionally social termination of pregnancy, while religious practice may moralize heavily. Neither approach may help a person going through a loss like this. Encouragement to forget the experience, or to feel perpetually guilty about it may not meet the case. For this reason some clergy offer rituals, as a way of putting the unsayable into action, for helping the people involved express the reality of what has happened, and appropriate remorse if necessary. This can also provide, for those affected by loss, the opportunity to continue in hope.

Themes which could usefully be touched in the ritual would include:

- An acknowledgement of the time the couple had spent together, and its significance in their shared life.
- Commitment to the continuing care and well being of the children of the marriage.

- Regret and remorse for the hurt that each may have caused the other – intended and unintended.
- Wishing the other well in their future (separate) life.[4]

A ritual to acknowledge a divorce may highlight shared memories, allow for a continuing commitment to responsibilities such as shared children, appropriate remorse and the opportunity to look towards the future. There is clear evidence from working with couples where a relationship is terminated by divorce or separation that 'unfinished business' from the previous relationship may affect the well-being of the current partnership. Both authors have been approached by people who have wished to have some sort of formal ending to their relationship. This helps them restore both their sense of responsibility and their dignity.

The Christian Church, along with other world religions, often has contact with people during the times when their lives may be undergoing great change, e.g. when babies are born, at puberty, marriage and when sickness and death become part of life. Pastoral care is particularly concerned with offering support, comfort and meaning to people who are undergoing change in their lives. In an important book, Clebsch and Jaekle[5] outline the historical background of some of the functions which are now taken for granted in pastoral care. They point out that one important element of care in the early Christian Church, in the time of persecution, was quite simply to offer the means for surviving and hanging on, the work of *sustaining*. Later came the issue of *reconciling* those who had fallen away under persecution. While the historical context is clearly different, the themes of sustaining and reconciling remain crucially important. It is deceptively easy to think that change produces quite straightforward feelings: gladness when something happens which is perceived as pleasant; and sadness when, for example, sickness or death occur. Feelings connected with change and loss are usually not quite so simple. Good care may consist of listening to, recognizing and understanding, words and feelings which may be contrary to the publicly expressed spirit of the occasion. To quote two examples:

A young man recently married went to see his minister because he felt that after six months of marriage he could not understand why he felt so trapped and sometimes quite sad in a partnership with a much loved wife. The minister, instead of encouraging him to think about what he had gained and how lucky he was, asked him what he thought he had lost when he got married. He began to talk with feeling about having lost his bearings. As he put it, 'The me I have had to live with until I got married has gone. I am never going to be the same again.' He found it was of immeasurable value to face the experience of loss and change as part of his adjustment to a marriage which he wanted very much to succeed.

A woman in her late fifties, whose husband died suddenly, was visited by a friend who kept mentioning how much she must have lost and how much she would miss her 'dear husband'. The newly-widowed woman became much distressed and later confided, to the minister, that the marriage had been a difficult one and that, although she missed her husband terribly in many ways, she wondered whether God would ever forgive her, for her immediate feelings on hearing of his death were ones of relief.

Every stage of growth carries with it the possibility of both benefit and threat. This was well described by a mother who, after the birth of her baby, exclaimed after a few, trying days, 'Will there be anything of me left?' – a sentiment which many would echo, not just in a maternity ward nor just connected with motherhood. H. A. Williams[6] describes death not only in terms of a physical body ceasing to function but also as the giving up of control, something which happens at many points in life. Giving up control is sometimes described as a 'little death' and can both involve a change in relationships, and also be part of the adjustment, for example, to a body which functions very differently after severe illness, accident or mutilating surgery, or even to the changed person who emerges from the experience.[7] The experience of sleep is frequently connected with death and is sometimes offered as a euphemism for it, frequently to the dismay of those who may connect sleep with death, especially if they have learnt prayers like, 'If I die before I wake, I pray the Lord my soul to take.'

So far, we have been looking mainly at those crises which are a normal part of our growth and which can to some extent be predictable. But there are other crises in life which Caplan[8] describes as 'accidental'. A child's pet may die. How the parents and other adults help the child with the crisis may affect profoundly the way in which he or she copes with other crises later in life. 'The child, when he first discovers that people die, quickly draws out the personal implications of the fact and, although in most incidences the effect of the original shock quickly disappears before the pressure of more immediate interest, the fact is duly registered by the mind and realisation of its fuller significance steadily grows.'[9]

Adults may seek to shield the child at all costs from the reality of death, even, in the case of a pet, to the extent of buying an identical animal in the hope that the child's pain can be alleviated or avoided, all in the belief that the child will be fooled by the deception. The child might be given an alternative explanation of the loss, the pet 'has gone away' or even 'gone to be with Jesus'. Studies made of explanations that parents give to their children about death suggest that 'religious' explanations are used almost as frequently by those parents who claim they have no religious belief as by those who claim religious allegiance.[10] The need to protect children from pain runs deep in the instincts of most adults. Children's literature, however, gives some evidence that it is fantasy rather than reality which is often hardest to cope with. (The story of *Beauty and the Beast* describes how the heroine faces up to her promise to marry the Beast, only to find that the Beast has become a prince. The fantasy of marriage to the old and ugly gives way to the excitement of the real person she discovers.) Pets may have, among their other important functions, that possibility of introducing children, and sometimes adults, to the experience of loss and grief in a painful but safe way when the pet dies. Terrible as the loss of a pet may be, it would normally be much less terrible in its implications than, say, the loss of a parent, brother, sister or friend. Many children seem to have strong instincts about doing the right thing around such events. One 12-year-old put it, 'The other day I saw a fox in the road and it was dead and we drove past it. That's wrong. You should always stop and say goodbye to dead things.'

Hospital staff, funeral directors and ministers may frequently meet people who in the middle of their life have not encountered death at first hand or even seen a dead body. But the way in which losses other than death are faced may be crucial, partly as an experience of living and maturing, and also as a struggling to understand the final loss which is one's own death.

Other losses can feel like a death or a series of 'little deaths'.

Michael had a stroke for which he was treated in hospital and which necessitated his leaving his managerial job and sitting at home. He became dependent on other people and he found it very hard to live with a body which, as he put it, 'no longer behaved'. He lost his status as a working person, as an active man, since he had to rely on his wife and daughter for much of his physical care, and he once described his experience as being a 'thousand-stage death'. He felt very strongly that his physical death was the last stage in a process and that he had been forced to let go his life in little bits over the previous two years.

Janet underwent extensive heart surgery and when she later came home told her friends and her minister that, while in hospital, she had had to face for the first time in her life the possibility of her own death and the knowledge that her body was not infallible. She had found this devastating since she had set great store by keeping herself healthy and making herself look attractive. She said, 'It was very hard for me to accept having to live in a body which was so diseased,' but she also saw her own coming close to death as something which made her rethink her life in terms of what was and what was not important.

Dorothy, a woman in her thirties with two pre-school children, entered hospital for the removal of a lump in her breast and found that, when she recovered consciousness, the breast had been removed. For two days she refused to mention what had happened and would not even look down at the site of the operation. However, she broke down in tears soon after her return home and told her husband to leave her since she was no longer, as she put it, 'a proper woman'. In challenging him she seemed to be asking him to do the thing which she most dreaded. She subsequently described the loss of her breast as like 'the beginning of the end'. She and her husband, with much support from friends, both came to recognize that their relationship would never be quite the same again and that it had to accommodate both the loss that had happened to her and the fact that she was suffering from a malignant illness.

Frequently, the treatment of some illnesses will involve the use of drugs, radiotherapy or surgery, which may alter very dramatically a person's physical appearance. A person may put on or lose weight, or their distribution of hair may change. A woman receiving treatment remarked that what had affected her most had been to look at herself in the mirror and to see, as she put it, all the hair in the wrong place. Sometimes the feelings which are connected with the change that illness or accident may bring about are described as 'change of body image'. Not only may the outside world appear a very different place and one's 'map' of that be changed, but more fundamentally, one's ability to live in one's own body may be considerably affected. There are no rigid rules about what one person may feel for no two people will have identical feelings about the same experience. But some sick people will experience frequent examination and medication, for example, as losing control over their own bodies, and that may assume as much importance as the illness itself. This need not necessarily apply just to people who are terminally ill or facing serious illness.

> Jane had a long history of miscarriages and realized that she would probably never be able to give birth to her own child. She described very vividly how she went through two or three days when she was thoroughly disgusted with her own body. She could not even bear to look at herself in the mirror since she felt so empty and useless. She did not like her husband to look at her either.

Such feelings usually pass, but it is important that they can be shared, if the person wishes. Most frequently help is best given by listening rather than trying to change the way someone else should cope. What most people dread is that their behaviour, following such losses, may be seen as 'irrational', whereas it is a very common expression of pain and confusion. Of course, the confusion may be felt by the sick person's friends and family as well, but possibly slightly differently. If a key person in a family, like a mother, becomes ill, her role can never be filled but her husband, relatives, friends and children may find themselves doing things to which they are not accustomed. She may simultaneously welcome the relief and also feel that her family may be managing too well without her, and she may experience resentment that she is no longer needed. Sometimes, if a person is ill for a long time, they may feel excluded from the family and feel that their role has been taken over by others. A man who, like Colin (in Chapter 2), is ill over a long period may feel very cut off from the rest of his family as they begin to take over the jobs he did at home and may also feel that he has lost his position as father and provider. Sometimes, in concentrating attention on a sick person, the needs of those close to him to grieve the loss involved in his sickness may not be so obvious, and only appear suddenly and sometimes quite dramatically.

> Graham, a young man paralysed after a road accident, was in hospital and a rehabilitation centre for ten months and his wife had visited him faithfully during that time. It was only on the day that he was discharged that she said very quietly as if she was not sure whether she could be heard or not, 'And will someone tell me what sort of a man they are giving me back!'

Her outburst was concerned, rightly, with herself and the profound changes, emotional, physical and sexual, which were implicit in her husband's condition. Very few of us live in such isolation that the effect of loss is confined to one person.

The 'little deaths' we have been describing provide part of the framework in which wider losses can be faced later on in life. They are not an exact preparation but to go through them successfully is to provide a framework against which larger and more fundamental losses can be faced.

Losses can be cumulative, and the experience of one loss can run into the experience of another. So it is never good enough to say that someone is 'overreacting' to a particular experience. An elderly lady whose husband had just died caused some concern to her family when she seemed not to connect with her husband's death but turned instead to her mother's death 60 years previously. It is important gently to help a bereaved or dying person identify what they experience as the significant loss, since this may not always be the apparent one.[11]

Notes

1 A. A. Milne, *The House at Pooh Corner* (Methuen, 1928).
2 Sigmund Freud, 'Mourning and Melancholia' in *Complete Psychological Works of Sigmund Freud*, vol. xiv (1914–16) (Hogarth).
3 J. Bowlby, *Attachment and Loss, Vol. i: Attachment* (Penguin, 1971).
4 A useful resource for such rituals can be found in H. Ward and J.

Wild, *Human Rites: Worship Resources for an Age of Change* (Cassell, 1995).

5 W. A. Clebsch and C. R. Jaekle, *Pastoral Care in Historical Perspective* (Harper and Row, 1967).

6 H. A. Williams, *Four Last Things* (Mowbray, 1960).

7 P. W. Speck, *Loss and Grief in Medicine* (Baillière Tindall, 1978).

8 G. Caplan, *An Approach to Community Mental Health* (Tavistock, 1969).

9 S. G. F. Brandon, *Man and his Destiny in Great Religions* (Manchester University Press, 1962).

10 G. Gorer, *Death, Grief and Mourning in Contemporary Britain* (Darton, Longman and Todd, 1965).

11 See C. M. Parkes, Joan Stevenson Hide and Peter Marris, *Attachment Across the Life Cycle* (Routledge, 1991).

FOUR

The Context of Dying

The death of a baby

Mary H came into the hospital for a normal delivery of her first baby. During the delivery of her baby she noticed that the atmosphere seemed to have changed and that the staff who were looking after her were rather different in their attitude. She did not feel able at the time to ask what was happening, but she sensed that something was wrong. She was placed in a side room in the maternity ward by herself. She wondered why, and asked her husband why she had not been able to see the baby.[1] It was only then that her husband told her that the baby had been born dead. Her first reaction was not to believe it and she insisted that the hospital had somehow confused the babies. Slowly the reality of what had happened dawned on her and she began to wonder why she had been so punished.

The birth of a baby who fails to survive is a much less common occurrence than it used to be, so that a still-birth, or the death of a baby in the first few days of life, is a shattering and unexpected event. Mrs H was not even sure whether her baby could have a funeral or not and she did not know how to approach a member of the clergy. The experience of losing a child early on in its life has been described by one parent as 'death before life' and it is against all the normal established order. Most of us expect to be survived by our children rather than to survive them.

In Mrs H's case, she was much helped by being taken to see the body of her baby. Some parents certainly do not want to do that. For parents like Mr and Mrs H the emotive experience of seeing the body of their baby gave them the opportunity of what one mother called 'seeing rather than wondering'. Fantasy about what might be is often more frightening than the reality of what is actually there. Most units in hospitals where premature or seriously ill babies are nursed will routinely offer parents a photograph of their baby. (Some even have a closed-circuit television linking the mother's bedside with the nursery.) If the baby lives the photograph provides the mother with some idea of how her baby is when she may not be in a position to see it; and if the baby dies it may be a crucial reminder to the parents that they did have a child with an existence of its own. A mother of a still-born baby described how confused she felt since it was hard to live with the memory of her pregnancy, the physical signs that her body was giving her,[2] contrasted with the fact that she had no baby in her arms. It was as if, she said, nine important months of her life had never happened, but she knew they had, and later she needed time to think about them and talk about them.

Mourning may not just be about things that have happened in the past but can equally involve possibilities that have not yet been realized. It is not uncommon for the parents of still-born babies and those who die soon after birth to experience profound feelings of self-disgust, as if somehow they had failed as parents and as people.[3]

Mrs H and her husband finally contacted their local minister who readily agreed to their request for a funeral for the baby. The service was simple and it was a sad occasion, but for the parents it seemed to recognize the fact that their baby's life had been a real one and that the 'chapter had been properly closed'. Even if a child is still-born it has still had an existence before its birth. The mother will usually have felt its movements inside her. Most Christian churches have now responded to our increased understanding of the nature of the life a baby leads before birth by being quite prepared to offer a funeral for a baby if this is what the parents wish.[4]

The sudden death of a baby at home, often in its cot and usually at a time when the parents are not present, is usually described as the 'sudden infant death syndrome'.[5] The parents will usually have had some chance to get to know the baby and to incorporate it into the life of the family. The child will have become a real and important person for its brothers and sisters and its other relatives. In legal terms this is a sudden and unexplained death for which, as a matter of routine, the police must be called and the coroner informed. Most police officers and coroner's staff handle the investigation of sudden infant deaths with great sensitivity, but the legal requirements may frequently compound the parents' sense of failure, that their ability as parents is somehow being questioned. A father whose baby died suddenly at home said, 'I had not realized that I would have to make a statement to the police. It was very illogical, but I kept thinking that they were going to ask me whether I had attacked the child. I felt so guilty and I knew that my wife did too. But at the time it was impossible to talk about.' Because of the circumstances in which most deaths of babies occur, it is extremely important to try to avoid, as far as possible, any approach which may sound as if the parents and the family are being judged, for most people in these circumstances feel guilty enough already.

There is a natural tendency if something terrible happens to think back on what one might have done to bring this about. One mother was terrified to mix the feed of her new baby because she felt that maybe she had not got the mixture quite right for her previous baby, who had died inexplicably in his cot. Some women may well experience a miscarriage early in pregnancy as a 'little bereavement'. It is usually of scant comfort to someone who has gone through the experience of a miscarriage to be told that it was early in their pregnancy so it could not have meant much. Here again, the issue involved is the facing of lost possibilities in a crisis. Most of us do not think logically especially when we are under stress. One task of pastoral care may be gently to support people who, for example, are connecting things they have done or thought in the past with some loss in the present. 'Is it something I've done?'[6]

What people are told when they are given bad news and what they experience may not always be exactly the same. It is very difficult to talk of 'abnormal' reactions to being given bad news. People may experience a powerful need to rush out of the room, or even to smile, or to block off and apparently not hear what they have been told. This is equally true for professionals such as medical, nursing and chaplaincy staff. Complaints are sometimes made by relatives about a staff member who was smiling all the time they were passing on terrible news. On investigation one nearly always finds the staff member was not aware of the 'mismatch' between their facial and body language and the news they were passing on.

An understanding of what would be culturally familiar is important. In some African and Chinese communities, people would not wish pregnant women and children to be exposed to grief, for cultural reasons which might extend to gender-specific reasons. Problems can arise when the individual's cultural and value system does not quite fit with that of their surrounding society, or the organization in which they are cared for, for example, a hospital or hospice.

There are a number of assumptions about how one is meant to behave in these circumstances, nearly always un-spoken! A natural, very human reaction to tragedy may be a 'magical' one. One woman whose baby had been stillborn said to her minister that this was her punishment for an earlier pregnancy which had been terminated for social reasons some years previously. The minister felt in a dilemma, as she did not believe in or wish to represent a God who would behave so crudely and punitively, but equally she wished to take seriously what was being said to her. She eventually said, 'I am sure that God is not punishing you, but I am equally sure that it feels as if he is.' That seemed to meet the woman's situation. But it illustrates the power of what we would call magical feeling and how important it is not to tell a bereaved or traumatized person that they should not think in that way.

Religion and magic may be confused, especially in grief, but it is important to maintain the distinction. Magical thinking is basically the belief that what we have said, done or thought has affected another person, and also affects the present. It affects how we deal, especially in a crisis, with the balance between what our 'inner world' and external experience may tell us. This inner world may involve reconnecting with voices and experiences from our past. The work of Joan Raphael-Leff has illustrated how fantasy can be particularly strong in the inner world of a pregnant woman, and links the interweaving of external and internal realities with the experience of loss and grief.[7] Even when alone, mental life has considerable substance, despite its 'imaginary' quality. Fantasies, even if they apparently defy reason, can be more influential in grief and loss than 'realities'. It is rarely helpful to challenge such fantasies by telling the bereaved or traumatized person that they are wrong. Part of them may know that what they are experiencing is not based on what they know in their heads, but equally this represents an area of our being which needs to be treated with care and respect. For example, much effort may be given to 'releasing' a person who in bereavement feels chronically responsible for the death of a loved one, without recognizing that giving up the fantasy that they might be in control would involve the person facing their own powerlessness and helplessness. The latter can be even more frightening and needs to be faced gently and with support.

The abnormal baby

Occasionally children are born with some sort of abnormality. This can involve a condition like a harelip or squint which can be corrected surgically, or a severe congenital disorder such as Spina Bifida or Down's Syndrome. The parents of a child who is severely handicapped have to face a double dilemma. It would be hard to imagine a parent wanting or anticipating the birth of a handicapped child. They have to face the loss, in the birth of their other than perfect child, of the perfect child who might have been. This can involve a lot of pain, in struggling to accept a child who is less than perfect, so the task of mourning may be two-fold.

Sometimes the feelings will be too profound to talk about and not everybody uses a framework of words to express them. The services which Christians offer round the birth of children, which mainly strike the theme of thanksgiving, may sometimes be used by parents of handicapped children as part of their way of coping with what has happened. A woman who had given birth to a severely handicapped baby asked for a thanksgiving service for his birth but turned up for the service dressed in black. The minister used a form of service with her which both thanked God for the birth of her child but also contained some prayers which picked up the theme of questioning God and how hard it was to accept something or somebody who was not exactly what was envisaged. Letting go of the image of the perfect child may be crucial for the parents, involving as it does facing their own limitations, before they can make any full acceptance of the child they have.

Death by suicide

On occasion ministers may find themselves in contact with those who have survived a suicide attempt and also with the relatives and friends of someone who has succeeded in killing themselves. It is not within the scope of this book to discuss in detail the pastoral care of the person who makes a suicide attempt. Interestingly, people who are terminally ill seem to have a low rate of suicide. Whether this is to do with life appearing very sweet if one is terminally ill or whether it is difficult for a seriously ill person to get hold of the means for killing themselves is a matter of some debate. Certainly, impulsive feelings about suicide seem common in some bereaved people, as part of their reaction to the crisis. Sometimes a person may attempt to take their life in the wake of a bereavement. Care of the people who survive when a family member or friend has committed suicide involves taking seriously the very powerful mixed feelings which often follow suicide.

Mrs R, a woman in her late thirties, found out after her husband's death that he had killed himself. She was both devastated that he could have done this to her as well as partly furious with herself for somehow making it happen. She felt that possibly, if she had been kinder or more understanding, her husband's death would not have happened.

The funeral service for her husband was important for her and the vicar tried to provide a service which picked up in its themes the very mixed feelings, as she put it 'of being either the murderer or being murdered', which she felt.

The feeling that something more might have been done seems particularly to pervade survivors when someone has committed suicide.

The care of a person or family or colleagues bereaved by suicide may involve taking very seriously the 'magical' feelings mentioned above. Their experience may well involve at one moment being bereaved, facing the loss of a person. At another moment they may feel at some level responsible for what happened, even if in reality they know that is not the case. At another moment they may experience themselves as the victim of a very savage assault because of the suicide; again, this is not a logical feeling. A natural reaction to being assaulted or hurt is perhaps to feel intense anger. The mother of a young man who committed suicide in a very premeditated way said to the minister at his funeral: 'If David were here, I could kill him for all the hurt he's put us through!' Then she burst into tears as she expressed her grief at the loss of a much loved son.

Some of the most difficult family situations one can imagine may involve the care of a family where one member makes a suicide attempt which will eventually lead to their death, but not immediately.

Mrs X, during a quarrel with her husband, swallowed weed-killer which was a slow-acting poison and she survived her attempted suicide for three days. During that time her husband and children alternated between wanting to go in to her hospital ward and cry with her and tell her that they forgave her, and getting very angry with the hospital who could not save her, and with the minister because God had not stopped her taking the poison. The situation was never completely resolved but the woman's daughter at her funeral commented that the 'poison was in the whole family'. With much support from friends and neighbours the family members began very slowly to be clearer about what responsibility was properly theirs, and what was the mother's.

Death in childhood and adolescence

For a person to die after the first six weeks of life is not now a common event. The circumstances in which a child or young person dies, at a time when he may 'have everything to look forward to', and frequently as a result of an accident or sudden illness, may make a particular and unforgettable impact on those who are involved.

Michael P was an 18-year-old man driving his fiancée home in his first car. They were involved in a crash in which his fiancée was killed instantly and Michael was taken to hospital seriously injured. During the time that his fiancée's funeral was taking place he was in the hospital's intensive care unit undergoing plastic surgery and his jaws were wired together. He afterwards said that, although he knew that his fiancée had died, it was still unreal for him. His friends visited him in hospital and afterwards when he was at home. They did not talk much together about the accident but at one moment thought of buying a plaque to place at the crematorium in the fiancée's memory, and at the next planning their football programme for the next season. It seemed as if nobody knew quite how the fiancée could be mentioned. Michael spent a lot of time sitting by himself and wondering why he had survived the crash when his fiancée had been killed. The health visitor who knew the family and the minister of his local church visited Michael regularly and showed that they understood his need to be angry at times with the other motorist involved, with himself for not having been more careful and for surviving his fiancée, and with the hospital who had not managed to revive her. By the time Michael had recovered he found it very difficult to make contact with his fiancée's parents but finally did so.

Adolescence is hardly ever an easy time for parents or for children and the sudden death of an adolescent child at a time when family life is often stormy can leave a very serious gap and many issues unresolved.

A mother of an adolescent boy killed in a motorbike accident bitterly reproached herself for the number of times that she had complained about motorbike parts being left in the house and wondered whether, if she had been more accommodating, her son might have made a better repair on his bike which might then have prevented the accident. Her son's youth club leader, who knew him well, helped her by remarking casually one day that he really had been a nuisance at times but that he was remembered in the club as a human being with strengths and weaknesses. The mother and father were slowly able to remember their son with the warmth of the relationship and also the difficulties in it.

There are conventions around grief which include the assumption that the dead person was always perfect, so it becomes impossible to speak anything but good of them. The reasons for the convention are quite clear and are rooted in the need to have something good by which to remember the dead person. But, equally, grieving involves putting together a set of memories of the person which bears some resemblance to the way that person was in life.

Children do not usually use a sophisticated system of words to describe their feelings and their world, and children who are terminally ill or bereaved are no exception. One small boy who had a tumour which was not responding to treatment was asked by his mother how he felt. He had certainly not been told that he was going to die but he immediately drew a tank with a little figure floating in front of its gun barrel. 'That's me,' he said. Caring for a child in a long terminal illness is one of the most exhausting and demanding tasks which can come the way of parents, brothers and sisters, other family members and those who have the professional care of the child.[8]

Mark G, a boy of 12, was admitted to hospital after the onset of severe headaches and was diagnosed with a brain tumour. During the last year of his life he spent some time at home with periods in hospital. He seemed to realize the serious nature of his illness and he made quite sure before his final admission to the hospital that his model cars and his Scout uniform went to people about whom he cared.

Samantha S, a little girl of seven, was admitted to hospital and soon afterwards sent home after an untreatable bone cancer had been diagnosed. The information was given to the parents, who did not discuss it with any other family members. Again she attended hospital for treatment. During the time that she was at home her mother found that she begrudged time spent with her other children and made a point of never being far away from Samantha. The other children in the family, who were older, remained outwardly well-behaved but showed other signs that they were resenting their mother's preoccupation with their sister. (Her elder sister said to a visitor that she would like to be ill too, since sick children saw more of grown-ups.) Samantha's father insisted that she was not ill at all and that if only the family could be rehoused and the children's damp bedroom changed, all would be well. Eventually the mother's and father's marriage broke down and the father coped by failing to visit Samantha in hospital and refusing to attend her funeral. He could, it seemed, only cope by rejecting the situation out of hand and Samantha's mother could only manage by involving herself totally with her daughter's care. It was as if the two parents between them were showing in their actions two extremes, of either getting so involved with a dying child that every other activity goes by the board or by denying the seriousness of what is happening. To try to find a middle way between the two extremes is very hard.

The pressures involved in caring for children facing death are huge. Pioneered by Helen House in Oxford, there are now a number of children's hospices, which cater for the special needs of dying and chronically ill children, and their families.

Increasingly care is given on a community or an outpatient basis. The opportunities for collaboration between the clergy and community-based hospice workers are considerable. In some countries the term 'specialist palliative care' is more acceptable than 'hospice', which has different meanings in some other languages.

Development of a concept of death

Children can be involved in the mourning for a member of their family. Sometimes this will be a brother or sister or parent. The way in which children slowly develop the idea of being dead and of death has been explored by Sylvia Anthony in an important study.[9] Small children seem to have very little conception of the permanence of death and are quite capable of talking at one moment about someone having died and at the next moment the possibility of their return.

> Janet, a four-year-old, whose brother had died suddenly aged 18 months, said quite simply, 'John is dead and we've buried him in the ground, but next spring we're going to find him.'

The sort of words used by children like Janet can be surprising for adults who may have seen her earlier, apparently much affected by the death of her brother.

Slowly, the growing child seems to achieve some awareness of the permanence of death. If children lose grandparents and relatives it may be important for them to have a chance to attend the funeral. Adults can often remember in later life occasions in their childhood when, in retrospect, they knew that a family funeral was taking place but at the time their attention had been diverted by a family outing, for example. It is often assumed that the worst thing that could possibly happen for a child would be to see parents and other relied-upon adults apparently deeply affected by mourning. But strangely enough, it may often be the denial of mourning in adults that children find most difficult to handle.

> A mother of two young children whose husband had died on the way to work refused to discuss the father's death with her children and told them simply that he had 'gone away'. The children subsequently in their play with other children in their neighbourhood mentioned that their

Mummy had cut their Daddy up and put him in little pieces in the ground.

However much adults may feel that they should remain strong 'because of the children', a child's experience of an adult who is sad and devastated but in the long run will be all right is usually much more realistic and reassuring than a blank denial of anything having happened.

The Children's Bereavement Centre at Alder Hey Hospital on Merseyside and the expanding work of the Child Bereavement Trust have helped to develop an improved understanding of the needs of bereaved children. The crucial role of significant adults who are in regular contact with the children, such as their schoolteachers, needs to be understood and developed.

Sudden death

There are clearly occasions when death is unprepared for, when somebody dies after an accident or sudden illness, such as a heart attack. In nearly all such cases feelings of *denial* are likely to be very important. 'I can't believe it's happened. I only saw him two hours ago.'[10] 'When we last spoke she was laughing and joking.' Frequently the feelings involved in the loss seem to take some time to catch up with the events, especially if a person dies in hospital. Friends and relatives may express bewilderment, frustration, sometimes rage, that more could not have been done. Again, there seems to be some evidence for thinking that those who have been involved in the care of the person in hospital in some way, even if only by sitting by the bedside or talking to an apparently unconscious person, seem to have some experience on which they can draw when looking back. The nursing staff in several intensive care units which treat patients with serious head injuries make a point of encouraging relatives to become involved with basic nursing tasks like lifting and washing the patient to help combat feelings of inadequacy.[11]

A three-year-old child was admitted to the hospital's intensive care unit following a road-traffic accident. She was placed on a life-support machine but was subsequently diagnosed as 'brain dead'. Her mother said, 'If only I could take her home. I feel so helpless.' She was not really asking to take her child home, but, staff believed, for permission to cuddle her. Her mother sat in a chair while the doctor, ward sister and chaplain helped lift the child off the bed (complete with tubes) onto her lap where she subsequently 'died'. The mother later said, 'She came into the world with a cuddle and went out with one. That was right.'

Death in disaster

In the aftermath of an accident resulting in the death of many people, mourning and feelings of grief may be expressed either by individuals directly involved in the event or corporately by groups or a whole community. This would include both the public and the private expressions of grief which might need to be attended to in different ways if a healthy outcome is to be achieved for all concerned.

Sometimes the impact of the public expressions of mourning within the local community, or the nation as a whole, may inhibit individuals from engaging with their own private grief,[12] especially if their private feelings are contrary to those being expressed corporately.[13]

Pastoral care after a major incident in which several people have died or been seriously injured together has been developed over the last ten years as an important dimension of care. In 1997 the Church of England published its *Guidelines for Faith Communities when Dealing with Disasters*. At the time of a major incident private and public expressions of grief can sometimes seem to pull in opposite directions. Both authors have worked in the aftermath of major incidents and found that the role of pastors was well accepted, once they were able to make clear their understanding of the professional boundaries and ways of working with colleagues in other disciplines. There seem to be three factors which make the aftermath of a major incident different from a 'smaller' event (although the significance of that event to the people concerned will be no less profound):

1 The sheer size of the incident and the fact that what has happened may not be immediately clear. We may find that seriously ill people and bereaved and traumatized people just keep coming. Communication between the site of the accident and those who are providing medical, nursing and pastoral care may not always be optimal.
2 The boundary between public and private grief may be difficult to maintain in view of understandable public interest manifested by the media. People who are injured or newly

bereaved may be interviewed in a way which exposes them. If for example somebody who has been bereaved says the 'right thing', or one person emerges as a hero they can be particularly vulnerable. Some communities hit by tragedy, as for example at Dunblane in 1996, are able with the help of significant community leaders, including clergy, to negotiate a withdrawal of the press and media and also of outside 'helpers' so that the community can manage its private grief.

3 The boundary for professional carers between 'them' and 'us' is much less easy to maintain especially if carers, including clergy, are part of that community. A natural reaction to disaster may be a quite appropriate sadness and thoughtfulness about what has happened and what really matters for an individual or a community. Carefully thought out memorial events may play a particularly important part.

People typically affected by a disaster might identify themselves as 'victims' as a result of their (real or imagined) involvement with the incident. Four types of victims might be classified as follows:[14]

'Event' victim	–	Those directly involved in the disaster.
'Contact' victim	–	Those who must exist within, or deal with a destroyed/devastated community.
'Peripheral' victim	–	Person with contacts/ties with the disaster area, but not directly involved in the event.
'Entry' victim	–	People searching for relatives, volunteers, professional helpers who enter the disaster area later.

The concept of *post-traumatic stress* can be very useful, if properly understood and applied.[15] It distinguishes between the completely 'normal' and predictable reactions which any person might have on being exposed to something shocking and unfamiliar, such as being involved in an accident where there are many casualties or being a 'carer' under these circumstances. But there is a difference between the normal post-traumatic syndrome, which is where the feelings listed below last for a period of approximately one month and then slowly recede, and the experience of post-traumatic stress disorder, the symptoms of which last longer and can affect day-to-day living in the long term. In examining post-traumatic stress it is possible to see its links with bereavement theory. We can talk in terms of four elements:

1 The person needs to have been involved in or exposed to something way beyond their normal experience.
2 The circumstances of the loss are re-experienced in a vivid way as if the event was taking place again – sometimes called flashbacks.
3 Numbness and a marked decrease of interest in everyday activity, feeling detached from others and not able to feel happiness or sadness.
4 Sleep disturbance, feeling 'high', being busy all the time and feeling jumpy at unexpected noise or movement. Feeling bad to have survived the experience when possibly others didn't. Difficulty in concentration and memory. Avoiding any activity which may feel linked with the event. Finding the feelings are reactivated on hearing of a similar event or when, for example, an inquiry or legal proceedings take place.

The specifics of pastoral care after a major incident are dealt with in a number of works. The important thing to remember about people who have experienced a disaster is to think in terms of a normal person to whom something highly abnormal and intrusive has happened. This means that the need for a person's boundaries to be respected becomes even greater. In the aftermath of disasters and traumas some workers and therapists have used a technique known as 'flooding'. This technique, as its name implies, seeks to expose the person to some of the sensations, memories and experiences which they went through in order to obtain some resolution of their feelings. It is important to stress that this overriding of a person's natural psychological defences carries a considerable element of risk, which can only be justified if a useful outcome can be foreseen. It is quite possible that the inappropriate use of 'flooding' by people who may not be aware of its consequences or who do not have access to appropriate psychological and psychiatric points of referral may do much more damage than good. It is certainly *not something to be attempted by clergy or ministers working on their own*. If this working has any benefit it is only when performed with care and with close supervision, allowing for the possibility that some of the people involved may require short-term, intensive psychological care.

Death in old age

Mr and Mrs T had been married for 52 years and they still remembered and spoke warmly of their golden wedding which had been attended by their children and grandchildren. Mr T used to make them both a cup of tea every morning and on the morning of his wife's death he had gone downstairs to make the tea and when he came back found that his wife was not breathing. He described his first feelings as 'just not being able to believe it'. The family doctor was called and confirmed that Mrs T had died suddenly in her sleep. The doctor had suggested that the local vicar should be contacted and although Mr T said he was 'not a churchgoer' he agreed to this. In the meantime, two neighbours had come and had laid out Mrs T's body. Mr T's reaction on seeing his wife's body was to say quite simply, 'It is her but it is not her.' His children arrived during the day. They lived in an adjacent suburb and wondered whether Mr T was 'up to' arranging a funeral and were very concerned to take the burden of practical arrangements from him. They asked the family doctor to prescribe a sedative for Mr T. The doctor refused, but said that if after a week or so Mr T had difficulty sleeping, he would be happy to prescribe something to help him sleep. Mr T's children were also very anxious that he should leave the house immediately and live with them. He was very reluctant to leave the house that he had shared with his wife for 42 years and said that he wanted to be with his memories for a while. He said that, although he knew she was dead, he expected to see her come downstairs at any time. (Such feelings are common.) The minister came on the day of Mrs T's death and, unlike the expectations that he would say a lot that was comforting, he listened to Mr T and asked him about the early stages of their marriage, where and how they met, and Mr T soon found that he was talking about events which were well in the past but which he remembered with surprising vividness, even down to details of the dress that Mrs T was wearing when they first met. He found it comforting to be put in touch once again with happy memories.

Mr T attended his wife's funeral and lived for a while

with his daughter but insisted that he could look after himself at home. Two years after Mrs T's death he still kept a place in the house that he described as her special place and a time of each day in which he remembered her there. The minister stayed in frequent contact with him and a lay visitor from the parish went in to see him every week or so.

It is very easy to assume that an elderly person has 'had a good life' and to offer this as a comfort to their relatives. But by the same token, if a person has lived for a long time, they may have become a key person in the lives of many people who will not have known life without them. In Mr T's case, his wife had been part of his life for all but 20 years of it.

Grief process

The process of grieving, as we have suggested, has similar features whatever the nature of the loss. But the circumstances in which the loss occurs, and other events in the life of the people involved, may highlight particular aspects. The importance of seeing the loss in the wider context of the person's life span is illustrated in Figure 2. This chart follows the way in which in an imaginary situation a wife experiences her grief when her husband dies. It sets out the important landmarks in her life and suggests how grieving for her husband may involve her recalling and re-examining those landmarks.

We have envisaged Mrs K in late middle-age, with grown-up children and grandchildren. Mr K was of a similar age to his wife and he has just died suddenly in hospital. On being told of her husband's death Mrs K's first reaction may be a denial, 'He can't be dead, I only saw him a short time ago.' Her 'if onlys', perhaps wondering whether things might have been different had, for example, she not left the ward briefly or had a particular nurse been on duty, are typical of those expressed by many people, especially as they begin to grasp the full impact of what has happened.

All she may be able to do is to keep repeating how good a husband he was, possibly expressing open bewilderment or anger that such a thing could happen to someone who was so good. She may ask why it has happened in a way which is more likely to be a statement of her pain and confusion than a question that has to be answered. If she is given the opportunity to see her husband's body, and accepts this, she may be able to make some distinction between the husband she

	PRESENT	Husband ill – comes into hospital	Middle age – birth of grandchildren	Children growing up – returns to work	Birth of children	Young marriage	Courtship	Adolescence	Childhood	Infancy
I can't believe it. I only saw him a moment ago		▨								
If only . . . he was such a good man . . . Why?		▨								
Sees husband's body		▨								
Yes it is him . . . I know it's happened . . . but . . .		▨▨								
When our first grandchild was born . . .		▨▨								
When we had to learn to live again as a couple when the children left . . .		▨▨								
When I went back to work . . .		▨▨▨								
Arrival of relatives		▨▨▨								
When our children were young . . .		▨▨▨▨								
When our children were born . . .		▨▨▨▨								
When we first married . . .		▨▨▨▨▨								
When I first met him . . .		▨▨▨▨▨▨			RECOLLECTIONS OF EARLY LIFE AND EARLY LOSSES					
Tentative steps into the future ◄		▨▨▨▨▨▨▨▨								

Note: The "LIFE BEFORE MARRIAGE . . ." band runs vertically through the Courtship column, with arrowheads (►) pointing left at the grandchild and relatives rows.

Figure 2. Grief process

remembers and the reality of his death. She may well say something like, 'Yes, it is him, but he isn't there.' Figure 2 shows that as time goes on she seems to be talking and thinking about events which increasingly give rise to memories from her past. Although it may seem to those with her that this is happening in a very random way, and indeed others may try to stop her becoming 'upset', there is more of a pattern to her feelings than appears at first encounter. We would *not* wish to say that the figure gives a universal method or 'technique', but we are continually struck by the number of people we meet whose grief seems to develop in a way which parallels Mrs K's.

The present time in the figure is marked by the first vertical column on the left. Everything Mrs K remembers from her past will inevitably come back to the present and the fact that her husband is dead. Her future is much too unsure (or in the terms of Figure 2, 'unmapped') for her to contemplate except for a very short time. Her relatives, who are also themselves having to face the loss of, say, father, uncle or brother, may try to encourage her to plan for the future but even two hours ahead is probably too far for Mrs K to imagine. One newly bereaved widow described the process of looking at the past she had shared with her husband as 'taking out the events of our shared life and then putting them back on the shelf'. This is exactly what Mrs K is doing. She remembers the time when her children left home and how it affected her marriage, what it was like to begin working outside the home again when her family had grown up. Even further back, she may surprise herself and recall the very early days of her marriage when her children were babies and also when she and her husband first met. For her to recall these events will be painful and poignant but it also seems to be for her a healing experience. She will probably be helped by what we would call 'lubricating' questions (e.g. I don't think you told me where you first met?) rather than 'change of gear' questions (e.g. Where are you going to live now?). It is possible that the marriage may have been difficult for Mrs K at some point, for example she may have felt that her husband had an unsatisfactory relationship with one of their children. She may wish to remember and talk about the times which were happy and those which were less than perfect, and by doing this help herself remember her husband and her marriage in its completeness. As she relives the events of her life the point will come when she will naturally remember, when she was a young woman, the time when her husband entered her life. The early events of her life, infancy, childhood and adolescence, did not involve her husband. It may well be that until, very slowly, she can 're-own' the married part of her life, the emotional resources on which she can rely are those which belong to a much earlier time in her life. Mrs K may well remember and relive other losses, deaths of parents, siblings or relatives, which took place a long time before but which may be vividly remembered with much feeling. A 75-year-old widower whose wife had died two days earlier told one of the authors that he felt 'like a lad of 19, but that's all wrong!' It turned out that this had indeed been his age when he had met his wife. Not every bereaved person speaks of such feelings but they have been common enough in our experience to justify mentioning them.

Only when Mrs K has gone back over her life and remembered, even re-experienced, some of its most crucial events, may she be able to make her first tentative steps into the future. In the interests of simplicity Figure 2 tabulates the course of feelings which, of course, never take place quite so neatly! The bereaved person's age, sex, cultural background, previous experiences of loss and the nature of their relationship to the dead person are all variable factors (see Chapters 1 and 3). There may be other reasons (see Chapter 6) which may delay or may inhibit mourning. Grief may also be inhibited or facilitated by the appropriate use of ritual and an understanding of the cultural setting.

Figure 2 picks up the emphasis on 'story' and its role in bereavement which Margaret Stroebe and others have developed. This illustration, which first appeared in the original edition of this text, in some way foreshadowed the 'story' approach developed by Stroebe and Hansson.[16] Its limitations may involve the difficulty of using this model by people who may not be verbally articulate and who might see this way of working as contrived. Stroebe also points to interesting possible differences between genders in coping with grief as part of her description of the 'dual-process' model. In summary, she suggests that women may need help in bereavement through connecting with concrete realities and activities, while men may need help confronting feelings and use activity as an escape from feeling.

Notes

1 J. Cooper, 'Reactions to Stillbirth: End this Conspiracy of Silence', *Nursing Mirror*, 149, 23 (1979), pp. 31–3.
2 A mother whose baby dies or is stillborn will undergo exactly the same physiological (and most of the psychological) reactions as if she had given birth to a live baby (e.g. the secretion of milk). She will usually be prescribed a course of tablets to suppress lactation.
3 Health Education Council pamphlet, *Loss of your Baby* and SANDS leaflet *Saying Goodbye to your Baby.*
4 If the baby is born in hospital, the parents can be offered a choice whether they arrange a funeral of their own or whether they wish the hospital to take over this function (see ch. 5, p. 87).
5 L. Clapp and J. Price, 'A Review of Sudden Infant Death Syndrome', *Journal of Nursing Care* (March 1980), pp. 13–17, 24.
6 P. W. Speck, 'Easing the Pain and Grief of Stillbirth', *Nursing Mirror* (25 May 1978).
7 J. Raphael-Leff, *Pregnancy: The Inside Story* (Sheldon Press, 1993).
8 Lindy Burton (ed.), *Care of the Child Facing Death* (Routledge, 1974).
9 Sylvia Anthony, *The Discovery of Death in Childhood and After* (Penguin, 1971).
10 See Figure 2 on p. 66.
11 P. W. Speck, 'The Hospital Visitor', *Nursing Times* (5 July 1973).
12 E. Lindemann, 'Symptomatology and Management of Acute Grief', *American Journal of Psychiatry* (October 1944).
13 A powerfully argued paper, 'Wounds of the Fathers' (H. A. Barocas and C. B. Barocas, *International Review of Psychoanalysis*, 6 (1979), pp. 331ff.), describes the private grief of concentration camp survivors, for whom no public expression or recognition of the enormity of the Holocaust was ever possible. But the next generation, the survivors' children who had been born after the war, seemed to display the symptoms of their parents' unexpressed grief. See also J. G. Edwards, 'Psychiatric Aspects of Civilian Disaster', *British Medical Journal*, 1 (1976), pp. 944–7; and J. Miller, *Aberfan – Disaster and its Aftermath* (Constable, 1974).
14 Adapted from S. W. Dudasik, 'Victimisation in natural disasters', *Disasters*, 4 (1980), pp. 329–37.
15 See F. Parkinson, *Post Trauma Stress* (Sheldon 1993) and M. Scott and S. Stradling, *Counselling for Post-Traumatic Stress* (Sage 1992).
16 M. S. Stroebe, W. Stroebe and R. O. Hansson, *Handbook of Bereavement: Theory, Research and Intervention* (Cambridge University Press, 1993).

FIVE

Rites and Customs

Introduction

It can often be difficult to know what to say or do when a crisis occurs, since our usual means of coping may seem inadequate. Therefore, all societies have developed forms of *ritual* which are built into their culture and provide acceptable ways for someone to behave in a disturbing situation.[1]

One very important group of ritual actions is that associated with life crises, which mark the passage from one social or religious status to another,[2] for example, the rituals relating to birth, marriage and death. One of the early major studies of these rituals was undertaken by Arnold van Gennep (1873–1957) who first employed the term *rites of passage*.[3] He saw these rites as a means whereby individuals might be eased, without undue social disruption, through the difficulties of transition from one social group to another. In this way Mary, whose husband had recently died, would make the change from being 'wife of John' to being 'widow of John'. Arnold van Gennep proposed three distinguishable and consecutive stages in this process:

Separation	or	Pre-Liminal	(before the threshold)
Transition	or	Liminal	(at the threshold)
Incorporation	or	Post-Liminal	(past the threshold)

The person, or group, on whom the rite focuses is first symbolically separated from his or her old status, then undergoes adjustment to the new status during the period of transition. Finally there is incorporation into society with a new social status. The relevance of these three parts of a rite of passage will be discussed further in connection with the pastoral care of the dying and the bereaved. It is important to note that the rituals associated with the care of the dying and the bereaved, and the disposal of the dead, do not replace the grief process. Rather the ritual is offered as a helpful structure or framework. If a ritual, or rite of passage, is to be relevant and aid the normal process of grief then it should meet needs at three levels:

The Psychological Level – by giving a framework for the full expression of feeling (grief) and to reduce anxiety.

The Theological or Philosophical Level – by which one seeks to make some sense and meaning out of what is experienced, in relation to the goal one is aiming for.

The Sociological Level – through sharing the experience with others and being re-accepted into society with a new status.

We shall consider the place of ritual in the grief process under two broad headings:

- Prior to the death.
- Following the death.

The place of ritual prior to the death

Making the relationship

Ideally our ministry to the dying person will have commenced long before the closing stages of life are reached so that we do not come as a complete stranger. This is equally true whether we are ministering to the person at home or in hospital. Sometimes we are called to a family or an individual in an emergency and there may be little time to build a relationship. Here one has to respond sensitively to the needs of the time and, if you do not know the family, remember they may see the minister as the forerunner of the undertaker!

Our previous knowledge and relationship with the dying person can influence the way in which we minister to them at the close of their life. To represent mortality is not always oppressive or frightening. Some of the people visited are very aware of what is happening to them and look to the clergy as people who are not afraid to talk of death. Ministers are also seen as people able to offer comfort and the reassurance of

God's love as well as enabling people to 'die well'. This help may be offered through a relationship and through the use of familiar ritual and liturgical forms. Not everyone is familiar with a sacramental ministry and so there is a need for flexibility in the forms of worship used. There may also be people who wish to see a minister but who have had little or no contact with 'the church' for very many years, but still feel anxious about what is happening to them. They often do not know what they wish the clergy to do but they hope that the minister will be able to sort it all out. It is as if, like 'instant coffee', there is an expectation that the minister can provide 'instant faith'. Much teaching may be necessary with both the family and the sick person if unreal expectations are to be avoided.

In that we must all grieve our own grief so we must do our own dying, and face the possibility and reality of our own mortality, and others should enable us to do this in our own way. A very fundamental source of anxiety for many is what will happen to those left behind and what will the process of dying be like. Sometimes a dying person will ask to be *helped* to die. The work done in hospices and elsewhere shows clearly that such requests arise when a person's pain is not being properly controlled or when people are not listening or responding appropriately. The request for 'mercy killing' is frequently a challenge to care and an expression of unmet needs.[4]

Sometimes the anxieties of the family and their reluctance to face the reality of impending death will create obstacles for the clergy. A wife may stay in the room all the time and give little or no opportunity for the minister, or dying man, to talk about what is happening and what he feels. It is sometimes easier to talk to the patient privately in the hospital than it is in the home if the relatives are not accepting of the patient's need to talk to a minister alone. This also applies to the relative as well as the dying person. The clergy may need to listen to simultaneously different needs. Because of their differing needs the relatives may 'protect' the patient from the minister because *they* cannot cope.

It is difficult to give set sayings for people to use in order to establish a more open relationship. One has to respond sensitively to what is happening and pick up what is conveyed in a look, a squeeze of the hand, a closed fist or eyes filling with tears. One has to listen to what is not said. To use a set opening sentence will usually guarantee that it will go wrong! If the person is anxious and upset one can sometimes ask, 'What did the hospital, or the doctor, have to say?' and then perhaps, 'What do you make of it all? How do you feel about that?' In some instances it may seem right to say, 'You seem upset today, are you in pain or are you feeling frightened?' These approaches allow the person to open up about their feelings and reactions to what is happening. If they do not wish to share their feelings, an open-ended approach allows the person to say, 'No, I'm fine,' and change the subject. We should avoid statements which corner the person or give them no let out.

The person who is dying grieves for the *impending* loss of their own life, in proportion to their awareness of what is happening. Therefore, we must expect to see and share in many of the normal grief reactions, already described, experienced by the dying person and the family. Death is not a single event but a process by which various functions of the body 'go to sleep'. Even after death has been certified, for example, the nails and hair continue to grow. The dying process, therefore, is one of gradually letting go. For this reason many dying people sleep a great deal towards the end of their life and so withdraw from contact and communication with their family and others around them. While this is natural, relatives may not always understand it and try to rouse the person and engage them in conversation. This is another reason for the minister being involved earlier on in the illness so that relationships have been built, discussions concluded and he is now free to come and simply *be* with the person. It is often very difficult to just sit and *be* with someone, for we may long to *do* something. There can, however, be nothing more irritating for the dying than overbusy people who cannot keep quiet and hold your hand, but must keep 'plumping up' the pillows every few minutes and demanding to know if you are all right.

An important part of pastoral care is to learn the art of *being still* and *being with* people. Any ministry that we perform should, therefore, be in tune with the patient's condition at the time of our visit.

Simply being with the dying: hours together saying nothing: this is an ability which I dare say clergy should develop more than they possess it: the ability to sit with someone, saying or doing nothing. Not just sitting looking vaguely and vacantly about, just knowing that 'if I sit for half-an-hour I will have done my job': and not sitting with a sort of pious look – 'I am praying next to my patient': and not talking in a pious or impious way... this ability, just to sit and go deep, so deep in sympathy, in compassion, is showing that you do not need these discourses, that your presence speaks: that if there is a need, you can put a hand on the person and it will mean more than whatever you can say.[5]

What are our pastoral aims to be?

There are four basic pastoral functions which can be identified in the pastoral relationship.

To reconcile – With the dying and the bereaved this function is very important and the need for reconciliation shows itself time and time again. People need help to re-establish broken relationships between themselves and God and between one another, and frequently they need to be reconciled with themselves and assured of forgiveness.

To sustain – The dying person requires supporting and sustaining if he or she is to endure and transcend what is happening to mind and body. Here the ministry of word and sacrament can be especially important.

To guide – Many people look to the clergy at such times to guide them both in what to do and also in their understanding of the nature of God, the person of Jesus Christ, and the Christian understanding of life after death.

To enable growth – If the individual is to grow and attain true health/wholeness/salvation then the minister needs time. When time is not available, reconciliation should become the focus, coupled with the understanding that this may enable growth to be achieved through dying and death.

It is interesting to note that, although different terminology is used, these same basic pastoral aims are reflected in the *Book of Common Prayer* order for the Visitation of the Sick. There the priest is directed to establish with the patient:

1 Penitence – sorrow for wrong-doing.
2 Charity – by restoring relationships, making a will, settling debts.
3 Increase of the sick person's faith.

These pastoral aims will best be achieved in the context of a sensitive, loving relationship, so that the dying person comes to believe in God's loving acceptance as a result of our loving acceptance of them. It is envisaged that this relationship will extend to include those others involved in the care of the dying person. If the person is dying in hospital then there should also be good liaison between the parish priest/minister and the hospital chaplain.

Most faith traditions have rituals designed to offer direction and support to the dying and their family. These may be passages from the sacred writings of that faith tradition, or instructions as to what is, or is not, permissible with regard to aspects of care before and after death. The appropriate faith leader should be contacted in the event of uncertainty as to good practice, following discussion with the patient and/or family. The following section deals mainly with the Christian tradition, but those working in a multi-faith setting should be sensitive to different needs and establish appropriate links with the other faith communities as resources to consult with.

Bible reading and prayer with the dying

Out of our relationship with the dying may come the request to hear a favourite passage of Scripture. It is helpful to check whether the person has a particular version in mind because Psalm 23 in an unfamiliar version may either stimulate further thought or greatly irritate. Our aim is to minister to the other person's needs not our own!

Various authors have selected suitable passages of varying lengths which might be used with the dying, and the Bible Societies produce selections of attractive leaflets which can be left with people to use after your visit is over.[6] Because very ill people find it hard to concentrate, the passages should be short and preferably familiar. However, we must avoid the temptation to use such readings as a means of avoiding dialogue or as a quick-exit line. 'Well, Mr Smith, I'm sorry I cannot stay longer but do remember – underneath are the everlasting arms.'

Because of drowsiness or unconsciousness it may be difficult to communicate *verbally* with the patient. The drowsiness may be drug-induced and by asking the times of medication one can sometimes arrange to visit during a more wakeful moment. If the person is unconscious one should still direct one's attention *to* the person and not *over* the person to the relatives. One can never be sure to what extent a seemingly unconscious person can still hear. Therefore, one should seek to pray *with* and not over the patient. For the same reason, one should be careful over what is said in the presence of the dying, even if they seem to be asleep. To pray 'We *commend* your servant, Alice . . .' may convey the meaning of 'Go forth upon thy journey . . .' and cause alarm and not comfort because the meaning was not clear. One day one of the authors was asked to see an elderly lady who was dying. After a long conversation he prayed with her and then said that he would commend her to God and bless her. As he said, 'Into your hands, O Lord, we commend your servant, Sarah . . .', she quickly stopped him and said, 'No! Not yet, Vicar, I'm not ready to go.' On another occasion the chaplain saw a man the night before he died. He said, on leaving, 'I'll see you sooner or later.' The man replied, 'Later rather than sooner, I hope.'

Flexibility in the prayers we use, and the way in which we pray, is also very important. A very tired and breathless person would find joining in a lot of prayers, or a long litany, too exhausting. If the person cannot join in the prayers it is helpful to suggest that they 'listen in their mind and say aloud the Amen'. Joining in or listening to the Lord's Prayer is very comforting, provided we pick the version they know. If concentration is poor people become very upset if they get lost and cannot remember the Lord's Prayer and so are often glad to say it with someone else. It is important that an affirmation of faith be included in our pastoral care of the dying. Once again, if the dying person is too ill to recite a creed one can use short questions to which the person may nod the head, say 'yes', or squeeze the hand. Sometimes we may need to make the affirmation on behalf of the person when we know this to accord with their belief.

The Sacraments

Baptism

During the course of one's ministry to the dying adult it may emerge that the person has never been baptized. If it accords with the wishes of the dying person then arrangements should be made to prepare the person at home, or in hospital.

Janet was 21 years of age when she had her first baby. She had been receiving treatment for cancer of the face for six months prior to the birth of the baby and shortly after the child's birth moved into the terminal phase of her illness. The local vicar was contacted about the baptism of the baby and during his visit it emerged that Janet had never been baptized. After due preparation he arranged for a joint baptism in the living room of Janet and Bob's home, since Janet was too ill to leave the house. The service was truly a healing service. It not only spoke of incorporation into the Body of Christ, of initiation, but it also illustrated another aspect of a rite of passage in that it aided the grieving process for Janet, her family, and the local neighbours who were present.

In the hospital setting the chaplain may be contacted regarding the baptism of a seriously ill baby. The sacramental ministry in hospital is the chaplain's responsibility, though he will naturally co-operate with local clergy by informing them about emergency baptism or anointings performed. He may also contact local clergy regarding the follow-up of people with whom he has had special pastoral contact. Likewise, the hospital chaplain would expect referrals from local clergy of people with special needs and to be consulted if clergy wish to conduct some special ministry for patients at the bedside.

The usual criteria for mentioning baptism to parents in hospital is if the child is critically ill and may not recover, or if he or she is to undergo surgery or have tests which might pose a risk for them, such as cardiac catheterization. The decision should be that of the parents and not because of the anxiety of the others around. The parents, some of the staff involved and perhaps grandparents should be present if at all possible and one should guard against 'hole in the corner' ministry of the sacraments. Likewise instruction as to what one is doing is important to dispel thoughts of superstition or ideas of magic. Some parents may prefer to have a ceremony for naming and blessing of their baby if they are unable to make the commitment entailed by baptism.

In baptizing critically ill children, or dying adults, one is not saying that to die unbaptized is to be rejected by God. One is performing in emergency the rite that the individual or family would still have wished to be performed were circumstances different. In emergency, of course, any lay person may perform the baptism and nurses are usually taught how to perform Trinitarian baptism, and to inform the chaplain subsequently. A certificate should be issued and entry made in the baptism register. If the child, or adult, lives then arrangements should be made subsequently for that person to be 'received into church'.

Where a dying adult has requested baptism it may also be appropriate for the hospital chaplain to contact the bishop and arrange for him to visit the patient to administer the rite of confirmation at the same time. Clearly the parish priest or minister would make the same arrangements with the bishop if the person was dying at home. Once again, hospital staff should be informed about the arrangements if the patient is in hospital. Quite often the hospital catering officer will arrange for a cake if due notice is given!

Sacrament of forgiveness

If one of our pastoral functions is to assist reconciliation then it is important that the dying person should be instructed to examine their life and identify those areas where there is estrangement and pain. Some people will react strongly to the use of the word 'confession', while others will request the sacrament themselves. Those who dislike the term 'confession', will still often seek forgiveness and absolution, but may express this as a desire to 'put things right'.

It is helpful to invite the person to consider the state of their relationship with God, other people and themselves. One may then be able to help them to acknowledge areas where things are wrong, to express contrition and seek forgiveness. Because privacy is not always easy to obtain in a hospital ward it helps to sit close to the patient's head. Those who are used to administering Holy Communion in a hospital ward will know the sudden lull in the ward's conversation following the words 'I confess . . .' from behind a curtain! By sitting close one can often speak quietly, even to the partially deaf, without others overhearing.

Irrespective of churchmanship the movement towards

reconciliation is an important part of achieving a peaceful death. In our earlier discussion of *rites of passage* we recognized three stages:

1 Separation.
2 Transition.
3 Incorporation.

The sacrament of forgiveness is an important part of this process, for it enables the dying person to let go of some of the ties with this life. It also resolves some of the anxieties about leaving this life in order to 'go to be with God'. This part of our pastoral ministry therefore greatly assists the dying person's growth in life.

Sacrament of Holy Communion

The Viaticum (the provision for the journey) is the term used for the last receiving of Holy Communion by a dying person. It is right that those who have been used to receiving Holy Communion in life should be given the opportunity to receive it at the time of their death. In the Church of England, Canon B 15a allows for 'any baptised person in immediate danger of death' to receive Communion. Within the Roman Catholic Church, 'those in danger of death from any cause are obliged to receive Communion'. This may either be given on its own or, if time allows, together with the sacraments of penance and anointing.[7]

The form of service used and the manner in which Communion is administered will vary according to the condition of the patient. Sometimes members of the family can be present and can join in the service and thus receive the sacrament with the patient. The rule of fasting is, of course, relaxed. It is usual to shorten the service and to use previously consecrated bread and wine. It is often easier to carry the consecrated bread and wine in a double pyx than to use a chalice. At the time of the administration one can intinct a small portion of the host/wafer with the wine and place it into the patient's mouth. A sip of water afterwards can help the person to swallow. Alternatively a fragment of bread can be put into some of the wine on a spoon. If the person is unable to swallow or receive anything by mouth the person should be assured that all the benefits of Communion are received.

On occasion it may be appropriate to consecrate the bread

and wine in the presence of the dying person and family, but frequently the service has to be kept short. Where possible one should at least include an act of faith, an act of penitence, the Lord's Prayer, the administration of the consecrated bread and wine, and the blessing and commendatory prayers.

The Viaticum is thus seen as a very important rite of passage in that it is received by the dying person as a means of grace and strength to assist him or her in the transition from this life to a fuller experience of Christ's risen life.

Sacrament of anointing or unction

In recent years there has been a very necessary and right move to re-establish the practice of anointing as a normal part of the Church's ministry of healing. This has been aided by the move within the Roman Catholic Church to talk of the 'Sacrament of the Sick' rather than 'Last Rites'. Because of the special nature of this sacrament, it should be reserved for crisis situations in serious illness. Clearly the approach of death is *one* such crisis, but not the only one for which unction is appropriate.

If the person is to be anointed in hospital there should be close liaison between the hospital chaplain and the person's own minister, who may wish to be present or administer the anointing. Likewise the medical and nursing staff should be informed about the anointing and the family should be present if possible. The medical and nursing staff often appreciate the opportunity to share in the service.

The anointing may be administered following an act of penitence and before receiving the final Holy Communion, or may be performed separately. The oil used should be pure olive oil consecrated by the bishop of the diocese or by the minister himself in accordance with a recognized form of service.[8] At the time of anointing the minister dips his thumb into the oil and makes the sign of the cross on the forehead of the dying person. Sometimes the hands of the person are anointed also. There should be a piece of clean cotton wool available for cleansing the patient's forehead and the minister's thumb after the anointing. The wool should later be burnt. One form of wording for the anointing is:

N, in the name of the Lord Jesus, I anoint you with oil. May our Heavenly Father grant you the inward anointing of his Holy Spirit of strength, and joy and peace. Amen.

If the dying person is unconscious and unable to receive Holy Communion it may still be appropriate to anoint him or her. We can never be sure how much an unconscious person can perceive and be aware of. On one occasion a seemingly unconscious patient made the sign of the cross twice during the administration of the laying on of hands and anointing, to the astonishment of all present.[9]

In many cases it may be most natural to include the laying on of hands at the same time as anointing the dying person. This may either take place immediately prior to the anointing or as part of the blessing at the end of the service.

One of the important aspects of the laying on of hands is that it enables some people to be touched in a non-threatening, non-sexual way, which in itself can be very therapeutic. Often when communication is difficult making physical contact can be important, provided it is clear and not tentative. Aromatherapy and massage of head or feet can be very healing and restorative for many people, especially if they feel their disease has made them 'untouchable'.

If the dying person is a child who has been baptized, but not confirmed, within the Church of England, Canon B 15a would allow for the child to receive Holy Communion and/or to receive anointing and the laying on of hands. Whether the dying person is an adult or a child it is important that time is spent preparing the family, the patient and others involved, concerning the meaning of what we are doing. The directness of a child and the depth of spirituality that one can experience with children make this part of our ministry both challenging and rewarding. It is only preparation which can avoid the danger of the sacraments being associated with magic and superstition. Such occasions can be important pastoral opportunities for teaching people about the Church's ministry of healing. It can also enable us to help people to appreciate that death can sometimes be part of the healing process.

Death-bed marriages

When someone becomes aware that they are approaching death they may express a wish to be married before they die. Unfortunately novels and films have given the impression that if you break your leg on the way to your wedding you can get married in hospital instead. However, it is not as easy as that! Under the Marriage (Registrar General's Licence) Act 1970 there are specific arrangements for people who are terminally ill and who wish to marry. These arrangements are in addition to those which enable the Archbishop of Canterbury to grant a special licence for such a marriage to be solemnized according to the rites of the Anglican church.[10]

While clergy may in some circumstances remarry divorcees, the Archbishop's licence does not allow for this. Changes in the Marriage Act have made it easier for people to arrange for weddings in a wider variety of places. When the local registrar solemnizes the marriage in a hospital or hospice ward the patient and spouse may request a blessing on their marriage. This can take place just after the actual marriage or on another occasion in the hospital/hospice chapel or quiet room, or on the ward.

If such a marriage is undertaken it is advisable that the sick person make a will. This should preferably be drawn up by a solicitor, but if this is not possible clergy and staff involved in the care of the patient should exercise caution before agreeing to witness such a will or codicil to an existing will. This is especially important if they, or their church, or their employing authority – such as hospital, nursing home or hospice – are to be beneficiaries.

Commendatory prayers

At the time of the death or shortly before, it is appropriate to pray with or for the dying person and to commend them into God's loving care. There are usually at least two aspects to commendatory prayers:

1 Expressing confidence in Christ and his saving work.
2 Commending the dying to God's mercy and love.

While the focus of such prayers is the dying person, the prayers may also have the effect of giving comfort and reassurance to the relatives concerning the victory of Christ over death.

Short texts or biblical readings may be used, or a litany may be said by those present. This can enable the family to have an active share in helping the dying person to 'die well'. It is interesting that most of the major world religions read certain passages of their sacred writings to the dying so that they may be a source of inspiration in their last hours. Prayers may also be made that the person shall safely pass, through death, from this life to whatever life is envisaged as being beyond death.[11]

Two forms of commendatory prayer within the Christian tradition are:

Heavenly Father, into whose hands your Son Jesus Christ commended his spirit at his last hour: into those same hands we now commend your servant . . . that death may be for *him* the gate to life and to eternal fellowship with you; through . . .

Go forth upon your journey from this world, O Christian soul, in the name of God the Father almighty who created you. Amen.

In the name of Jesus Christ who suffered for you. Amen.

In the name of the Holy Spirit who strengthens you. Amen.

In communion with the blessed Saints, and aided by Angels and Archangels, and all the armies of the heavenly host. Amen.

May your portion this day be in peace, and your dwelling in the heavenly Jerusalem. Amen.

Increasingly people have no involvement with the Church or other organized religion. Nevertheless they may still have a real spirituality[12] and may look to chaplains or other faith leaders to help them find an appropriate way of saying goodbye at the time of death, if we can be flexible.

A 20-year-old woman was dying in intensive care. Karen had been ill for a long time with leukaemia and, in spite of treatment, the aggressive nature of the disease meant she would shortly die. Most of her friends were young and with no formal religious involvement. Karen's mother described herself and her daughter as non-religious but spiritual and asked the chaplain to help them in the final hours of Karen's life. In addition to her mother there were almost a dozen friends, all silent and many looking at the chaplain as if he had come from Mars. The chaplain explained that he was there at the mother's invitation and then spoke to several friends to try and establish where they were emotionally and whether they had said their goodbyes or not. Eventually it emerged that the most significant music for Karen was 'whale song' from the deep oceans. While the whale songs were playing each person was invited to say their goodbye in whatever way made sense to them. Some spoke into Karen's ear very quietly and privately. Others sat quietly and held her hand or feet. Some kissed Karen and then held each other. It became clear that Karen was sinking fast and it felt important to have some corporate acknowledgement. The chaplain proposed that, although people were not religious, perhaps they would feel able to share in the serenity prayer: 'God grant me the serenity to accept the things I cannot change, the courage to change the things I can, and the wisdom to know the difference' (Reinhold Niebuhr). Several of the group had had involvement with AA and Narcotics Anonymous, and it proved to be a truly uniting act. Whale song may not appeal to everyone but on this occasion it was absolutely right.

At the time of death

As a person approaches death the level of unconsciousness deepens and the pattern of breathing alters. Because of moisture in the chest there may be a rattling sound which can alarm people. The breathing may also stop momentarily and then suddenly start again. Eventually a moment is reached when the muscles relax and the last breath escapes from the body. The heart stops and the person becomes very pale and gradually colder. There may be some slight muscular movement after death and this can lead people mistakenly to think that death has not yet occurred. In a hospital a nurse will usually examine the person and then call a doctor who will verify death.

Death at home

If the person has died at home the family should remove excess bedding, leaving just one pillow, and lay the person straight. The mouth may be held closed by placing a suitable object under the chin, a pillow or book, and the eyelids closed. Heating should be turned off in the room and the doctor informed. The doctor will come to verify death and to issue the death certificate. The minister should be informed, and then the funeral director. If there is no contact with the church the family should contact the funeral director, who will help them make the necessary arrangements and remove the body from the home if that is their wish.

Washing the body is often undertaken by the funeral director, because nowadays not many communities have an official 'layer out'. The task of washing the body and laying out was often performed by a woman or group in the community who could be contacted by the family. This has traditionally been a task carried out by women as instanced by the women who came to the tomb on the first Easter morning to anoint the body of Jesus (Luke 23.55–6). This preparation is often seen as a sort of last service and act of love for the deceased and a member of the family may wish to assist when this is performed at the home, or in hospital. The laying out is often concluded with prayer. Some religious groups have special prayers and rites for this washing and only certain people are allowed to perform the ritual. In the Muslim and Jewish communities those not of the faith should not wash the body of a deceased person since a non-believer could defile the dead person. For this reason an orthodox Jewish family would employ a 'watcher' to stay with the body from the time of the death until the time of the burial. With a Muslim the head would be turned to the right shoulder so that the body can be buried facing Mecca.[13]

Brain stem death and organ transplantation

When the person has been receiving life-supporting aid prior to death, the definition of death may seemingly be more difficult. However, the British guidelines for the establishment of what has been termed 'brain stem death' have moved us away from only defining death as cessation of heartbeat. In spite of controversy, the tests laid down,[14] *if properly performed*, should lead to a clear diagnosis of 'brain stem death'. This is especially important if the family are to be approached, at a very emotive time, with a request for the donation of organs for transplantation. We do not feel that it is usually the minister's role to make such requests personally, but to accompany the doctor who makes the request and to be available to comfort and support the family at this time. On occasion, however, the chaplain may be the most suitable person.[15]

Relatives may ask faith leaders for guidance as to whether there are any religious objections to organ transplantation. Most faiths would see this as meritorious, though Judaism and Islam would wish the benefit to be assured in order to justify the violation of the dead person's body. Most Christians would agree on religious grounds, though emotionally they may have objections because they have not yet sufficiently acknowledged that the person is dead. Certainly relatives (and staff) can find it difficult when a patient who has brain stem death is transferred to the operating theatre on life-support while vital organs are removed for transplantation. The life-support is required to ensure the donated organs are in as good a condition as possible for transplantation. Head and heart may not always be in tune and relatives may require a reasonable period of time to elapse before they can cope with this. An opportunity, with or without a chaplain present, to say goodbye before the deceased goes to theatre can help relatives to recognize that the patient really has died even though looking asleep. Some recognition is needed that people can be at different emotional places in adjusting to the death or their ability to face reality. For this reason it will probably always be difficult to decide whether relatives should be present and witness the resuscitation of a patient. Some will find it comforting to know, and have seen, that everything possible was done if the patient dies. Others will find the experience, the noise, the visual images quite traumatizing. It is difficult to see how staff, who have very little knowledge of the family's coping ability, can decide who should or should not be present. Research and pilot studies have been undertaken in Australia, USA and in the UK, which indicate that where it is decided appropriate for relatives to be present it is advisable that a staff member be assigned specifically to those relatives in order to 'be there' for them while resuscitation is attempted. This might be a nurse or chaplain. There also need to be clear guidelines for staff regarding preparation of the relatives and their conduct in order to alleviate the anxieties of the staff.

Involving the coroner

In certain circumstances the doctor may not feel able to issue a death certificate and may need to report the death to the coroner. The coroner will then look into the facts of the case and issue the certificate when he is satisfied as to the cause of death. This procedure covers deaths certified as directly or indirectly due to violence. Deaths which are sudden, attended by suspicious circumstances, or whose cause is unknown, will also be referred to the coroner.

Stillborn babies

If the deceased is a stillborn child[16] the doctor or midwife will issue a Medical Certificate of Stillbirth, instead of a death certificate, which should be taken to the Registrar's Office within six weeks. A certificate of burial or cremation will then be issued to the parents as for any other person who has died. In these sad situations the birth and the death have to be registered. Parents can now have the baby's name entered in the Register. As one father said later, 'It was the non-event of the year!' Most hospitals make it possible for the parents of a baby who has been stillborn, or who has died in the first few hours of life, either to make the funeral arrangements themselves with a funeral director of their choice or to sign a form authorizing the hospital to arrange the baby's funeral. In the latter case it is still possible for the parents of the child to be informed of the date and time, and for them to attend if they wish.[17]

In the event of a spontaneous abortion (up to 24 weeks' gestation) or miscarriage, it is still possible to have a funeral provided the hospital, or the attending doctor, issue a 'certificate of delivery of a non-viable foetus' in lieu of the stillbirth certificate (a covering letter to facilitate arranging the funeral). Parents might also choose to have a simple ceremony or service in the hospital chapel or local church to enable them to say hello and goodbye to their baby. If parents choose cremation rather than burial it is important that they know that there will usually be no ashes recoverable for them to keep or bury. The Stillbirth and Neonatal Deaths Society (SANDS) publishes excellent guidelines for parents and carers on the various options and fostering of good practice.

Viewing the body

If the family were not present at the time of the death they may wish to see the body. This can either be in the chapel or viewing room attached to the hospital mortuary[18] or at the funeral director's chapel of rest. Sometimes this may happen in the ward of the hospital, as in the case of a stillbirth, where the parents may wish to see and hold their dead baby. It can be more natural for the person to be viewed either in the hospital bed or their bed at home, rather than in the starkness of a mortuary chapel or viewing room. One cannot lay down policies that everyone, or no one, should view the deceased. The next of kin has the right to see the deceased but the timing and place of viewing must be by mutual arrangement. In the hospital nurses should ask relatives if they wish a chaplain to accompany them when they view the deceased. Many relatives say yes and wish for prayers at such a time. There should be no rush at such times and occasionally staff may hurry relatives because they themselves are finding it difficult to cope. Viewing the body can help many relatives who are denying the reality of the death and so can be important for their subsequent grief work. While not everybody will wish to see the deceased the opportunity to do so should be given to them.

If the minister is accompanying relatives to view a body following a road-traffic accident or similar incident it is advisable for them, or someone else, to see the body first. This then enables them to prepare the next of kin for what they may see. This is important if there are facial injuries or other disfigurement.

Clergy are sometimes asked whether children should go to view the body of a dead relative. One cannot be dogmatic about this. It depends so much on the child and the circumstances of the death. If it is a peaceful death at home then, *if the child wishes*, it can best take place by the child accompanying an adult after the laying out has been completed. In this way the child can hold an adult's hand and see the deceased in bed in a more natural surrounding than in a coffin at the funeral director's, and in this way say their goodbyes. We cannot 'shield' a child from what has happened. Frequently a child who shares the distress of the family may be able to use the experience in later life. One has to balance the short-term distress against the long-term effects of maladaptation over what might be the next 50 years.

Request for a post-mortem examination

It is not easy to ask a family for permission to perform a post-mortem examination. Sometimes there is little choice because it is required by the coroner for medico-legal reasons. In fact in the Jewish and Muslim communities permission for autopsy will usually *only* be given when there are medico-legal reasons for it. In all other cases the next of kin has the right to say no to a post-mortem if they object to it. Some families find it very hard to distinguish between 'head' and 'heart' and so although they know the person is dead will withhold consent because 'he has suffered enough already and they are not going to cut him up any more.' On the other hand some relatives are willing to consent because they wish to know the exact cause of death, or need to know if the condition of a child is an inherited one (i.e. they consent in order to help the living). The request is usually made to enable the medical staff to learn more about the illness which led to the death or to teach medical students.

If consent is given for a post-mortem it will not usually delay things very much. Every care is taken to ensure that the face of the dead person is not altered so that the person can still be viewed subsequently. When contacting a funeral director it is important to tell him or her whether or not there is to be a post-mortem.

If the deceased had arranged in life for their body to be donated to the medical school's department of anatomy the medical practitioner at the hospital or at home should be informed prior to the death if possible. This fact should certainly be communicated before any post-mortem examination is carried out. It is important during life that people who wish their bodies to be given for dissection make the proper arrangements with the university department of anatomy, inform their next of kin, and understand that sometimes the cause of death or the removal of organs may lead the department to have to decline the offer. This can upset relatives if they have not realized the possibility of this happening. We shall comment later on the funeral arrangements in those circumstances (p. 102).

The place of ritual following the death

The funeral and associated events

The funeral is an extremely important event, since it can be the culmination of a process of care for the dying and the bereaved. The way we die is a reflection of the way we have lived. Similarly, the manner in which we dispose of our dead can be a reflection of our attitude towards death, and towards the person who has died.

The family of a faithful parishioner of the Anglican or Roman Catholic tradition who has died may express the wish for their body to be received into church the night before the funeral and for a requiem to be said. The actual funeral service would then be held the next day in the church, followed by committal of the body at either graveside or crematorium. In this instance the entire ritual is being set in the context of the worshipping community and is expressive of the life and belief of the deceased and the bereaved.

A family who have little or no contact with any place of

worship, and who find it hard to face death, may request a 'short service'. They may leave the funeral director to make arrangements with the 'duty man' for the service and will arrange to 'meet you at the crematorium for a simple service'.

In contrasting these two different types of funeral no judgement is being made about the sincerity of feeling among those attending the funerals. The contrast is more concerned with different beliefs and attitudes towards death leading to differing requests concerning funeral arrangements. Both of these families, however, will have need to do their own 'grief work', and, whatever their beliefs, the funeral ritual will either help or hinder that grief process.

We referred earlier to the work done by van Gennep and others on *rites of passage* and the importance of these rites to facilitate the transition from one status to another. The funeral service and the events surrounding it can be very significant for both the deceased and the mourners. If the ritual is to facilitate grief the family and the community must be involved in the three aspects of the rite of passage:

Separation – Transition – Incorporation.

These three aspects are not rigidly separated from each other, but are a convenient way of identifying what the rite can signify for the deceased and the bereaved.

Separation

When a death occurs there is inevitably separation which may be gradual or it may be a sudden wrenching apart. However it happens, the bereaved and the deceased must separate from each other and 'let each other go'.

Separation for the deceased

An important aspect of terminal care is assisting the dying person towards a dignified and peaceful death. If the minister has been involved with the dying person at this stage of their illness, then his or her pastoral care will have enabled them to say something about separation as well as reducing the anxiety of the dying. Being separated from those you love in this life raises the question of 'letting go into what?' This is a question about which clergy do have something to say.

While the commendatory prayers at the time of death have the prime intention of commending the dying to God's mercy and love, they can also act as a means of giving permission for the dying to die. It not infrequently happens that following anointing, prayer and commendation the dying person will visibly relax and begin to 'slip away'. It is as if they feel that permission has been granted to let go and, therefore, they can now 'go forth upon thy journey'.

Separation for the bereaved

The bereaved must allow the dying to die and, having died, to let them be dead. Hence the need to declare the deceased to be dead in any prayers or ritual at this time, since it can aid separation. This is especially true if there is no physical body to see and touch, as may happen if the person is lost at sea, or the body is donated to anatomy. Just as in the wedding service the priest says, 'I pronounce you man and wife together,' so in the funeral service he or she must declare the deceased to be dead, by not being afraid to use the words 'dead' and 'died'. Because of the shock and denial in the early part of grief we may need to restate the reality of death several times, either verbally or through such actions as seeing the body and thus saying 'goodbye'.

It can be quite normal, if somewhat disturbing, for the bereaved to believe they have seen or heard the deceased in and around the home. A sense of presence is quite common. However, this is quite different from deliberately setting out to make contact with the deceased through spiritualism. By trying to contact the dead in this way we are attempting to hold them back instead of letting them go. Sometimes it is because we feel guilty and wish forgiveness or understanding from the dead person. It may simply be that we are seeking reassurance that they are 'all right'. To a Christian to hold on to the deceased in this way shows a lack of trust in a loving God. Jesus said to Mary in the garden, 'Do not cling to me . . .' (John 20.17) and in the same way we must resist the temptation to cling. Rather we must allow separation to occur so that the departed is freed to go to God.

In some communities it is still the custom to draw the curtains at the front of the house from the time of the death until the funeral is over. This signifies to others that there has been a death and that the next of kin has withdrawn from the community and their normal pattern of living. It is also the cue for others to call and make condolence visits and offer help. The bereaved thus become *separated* in order to become the focus of care from both the family and the community. The placing of the 'death notice' in the local paper can be another way of bringing home the reality of the death even though the next of kin may not wish to look at it immediately. Similarly, condolence cards and letters are appreciated. While they may not be read properly until much later, they do signify the support and prayers of others.

With urbanization, rehousing and changes in the family structure, there are now many people who may be very isolated and receive little help at such a time. It has been shown[19] that in one sample of bereaved people, 37 per cent received no help with the funeral arrangements and had to cope with it all on their own. In some blocks of flats neighbours may not know that there has been a death until they see a hearse outside. Separation of the bereaved from the dead and from the obligations of their normal living pattern is a temporary state, but can serve to heighten loneliness if there is insufficient support for the bereaved.

Pre-funeral visits by the clergy

The prime 'funeral director' should be the minister, where he or she is already involved with the family as their parish minister. In that the minister will have cared for them during any previous life crises they will turn to the church for guidance and help and the minister for leadership and support to enable them to say and do things that 'feel right'.

Clearly there needs to be a good relationship and liaison between clergy and funeral directors. With those families who have no church connection the funeral director can fulfil an important caring role and may often pave the way for a visit by a minister whom they have not met. In many places clergy and funeral directors work closely together and, as far as possible, funerals are taken by the clergy who are likely to have continuing pastoral contact with the bereaved. In spite of the many jokes which connect clergy and funeral directors, their mutual understanding of each other's role and support for the bereaved can do much to enable growth from this pastoral opportunity. Where a death has occurred in hospital a referral to the appropriate minister by the chaplain (if they have been involved) can give a lead-in for this first visit.

The pre-funeral visit to a family where one is known and welcomed is quite different from that where one has had no previous pastoral contact. It is not usually a time for one-to-one bereavement counselling. There is often much coming and going, with relatives and friends in and out of the room, and the next of kin perhaps shocked and numb. To the family the main purpose for the visit is seen to be the necessity of arranging the funeral.

There will be discussion of hymns, Bible reading, flowers, burial or cremation, disposal of ashes, prayers at the house, and the meaning and form of service to be used. If the dead person has been brought back to the house this may lead to prayer with the bereaved in the presence of the deceased.

> Following the death of a three-year-old child in a traffic accident the minister found, when making a pre-funeral visit, that the front room had been cleared of all furniture. In the centre of the room was the little coffin, surrounded by toys, and people were taken in to say 'goodbye' to the child. The minister was also invited to 'see Anne' and thus given the opportunity to talk about the deceased, the reality of the death and to pray with the family by the coffin.

To pray or not to pray is a common question. If you ask the family they often say yes because they feel they should. A prayer should not be a means of wrapping it all up, silencing the family, or protecting the minister! There needs to be a spirit of openness which echoes and offers up to the love of God what has been shared in the visit – the positive and the negative, the rage and doubt, submission and bewilderment.

While there needs to be some discussion, there also needs to be time to listen to what is happening within the family. A home visit can enable one to build up a picture of the various and different reactions of family members, to assess where they are in their grief, and to gain information about the deceased. Various members of the family may be at different points in their grief which, coupled with previous rivalries, can lead to friction. Two sons may be competing to sort out mum's finances or it may be that the family is good at sorting out practical difficulties but not at coping with emotions. The extent to which the next of kin will be subsequently isolated when the family members return to their own homes may also be evident. It may also be possible to pick up whether the needs of younger children are being recognized, and whether they are being allowed to face reality.

As mentioned earlier, the family may feel angry with God for allowing the death to occur and to have seemingly brought about a separation which they did not want. While they need the minister to conduct the funeral they may resent his presence and intrusion into their territory, but tolerate the visit.

On the other hand they may feel the need to impress on the minister what a 'good person' the deceased was and therefore worthy of a good funeral. This may be coupled with a readiness to accept whatever is suggested, even if it is not exactly what they feel, as if to placate the minister (or God) for previous non-attendance at church. Listening can help to uncover some of these ploys and to bring things back to a more realistic level. Discussion about the deceased and some of the good and bad experiences shared can be relevant and helpful on occasions if done sensitively. Discussion of the illness and the death may also help in putting the bereaved in touch with the *real* person from whom they have been separated.

The pre-funeral visit not only serves to prepare the family for the funeral, but can be important in aiding the separation because of the authority and status of the minister on such occasions. The visit also has the effect of preparing the 'agenda' for subsequent pastoral care at the funeral and later, and of communicating God's loving care at a time of pain and sorrow.

Transition

This is an in-between time while, for example, Mrs Jones *wife of* . . . becomes Mrs Jones *widow of* . . . . She may feel a stateless person until a new identity or social role has been formed and accepted. Likewise a couple whose child has died may feel the loss of the status of 'parent'.

Transition for the deceased

The transition for the deceased is related to the anxiety expressed by many bereaved people as to where the dead person has gone to. The concept of a journey is prevalent with many people and there can be great anxiety about 'hell, limbo and heaven', often disguised in jokes about 'Harry always being good with a shovel . . .' and strong feelings about cremation and the language used at the committal. Linked with this can be the anxiety that the dead in some way may be able to do harm. 'Never speak ill of the dead' has overtones of fear of reprisals as well as genuine respect for the departed. The obverse is sometimes seen with divorce where some may speak only bad of the divorced spouse. Public recognition of the death of the deceased is an important part of the transition, linked as it is with the public recognition of the length and value of the life of the individual. Such praise for the deceased may have the effect of assuaging guilt felt by the mourners, while also saying to God, 'Here is someone worthy of your attention.'

What we should be seeking to express at this time of transition is our faith and hope in God's love and grace, and not in what we have achieved in life. Eulogies, elaborate arrangements and sentiment can sometimes cloud this for us, whereas a genuine act of thanksgiving for the deceased and the family may reaffirm our dependence and trust in God.

An important part of liturgy, therefore, is to reaffirm the continuity in Christ of the living and the dead and the appropriateness of commending the departed to the mercy and love of God. For many it is the Eucharist and the Requiem which symbolize this most clearly. It may seem something of a paradox to the onlooker to see a practising Christian, at the funeral of a loved one, joyfully singing, 'Thine be the glory' with tears streaming down the face. However, there is a joy in knowing that the deceased is with God while at the same time grieving for the loss of their physical presence.

> I am sure that neither death, nor life, nor angels, nor principalities, nor things present, nor things to come, nor powers, nor height, nor depth, nor anything else in all creation, will be able to separate us from the love of God in Christ Jesus our Lord.[20]

Transition for the bereaved

> The interval between the decay of the old and the formation and the establishment of the new, constitutes a period of transition, which must always necessarily be one of uncertainty, confusion . . .[21]

For the bereaved the transition phase of the rite of passage is the time when the past is left behind and the future has not yet begun. It is the period between Good Friday and Easter Day. One's point of reference has gone and time seems to stand still as an endeavour is made to discover and accept a new identity and status. There can be much uncertainty and confusion as one looks to friends and family for help and support in adjusting to a new status as 'widow, orphan, single person'. The funeral ritual and associated events are a vital part of this because the funeral has the capability of encapsulating the full process of separation, transition and incorporation and thus enabling the bereaved to move forward in their grief. It does not do the grief work for them, but it can act as a catalyst. The extent to which the ritual achieves this aim of stimulating grief work is dependent upon several factors: what is done before the funeral service, the attendance and support of the family and friends, the individual character of the bereaved, and the level of actual involvement of those attending.

Family and friends

Several studies have been undertaken which have shown the importance of the funeral as a gathering of the kin and friends of the deceased.[22] There are regional differences in that the funeral and the gathering in the home afterwards have a much higher attendance in Scotland, Wales and northern England, than in the south of England. The findings indicate that there needed to be an obligatory occasion to make them visit.

The presence of the family and friends at the funeral service and at the house is comforting and also aids the acknowledgement of the new status. One study[23] suggests that 'the *bereaved* are comforted by the presence of *close kin* at that time and derive their sense of support from this and the general gathering, whereas it is the *other kin* who obtain a sense of solidarity and a reinforcement of kin relations by noticing in detail whom of their number attend.' The help given by the family and friends can serve to reassure the bereaved that they will be acceptable in their new role and status. One survey investigated various ways in which family and friends helped the bereaved following a death,[24] and the results are summarized in Table 2.

In addition to the help listed in Table 2, 30 per cent of the surveyed group received financial help with the cost of the funeral. It is also significant that this same survey showed that most of the help given was practical rather than passive/emotional support, and that 37 per cent stated that they received no help at all. The presence and support of family and friends, both at the funeral and subsequently at the house, is something appreciated by the bereaved even if the motives for coming may be suspect in some instances. If the bereaved are to be aided in moving from old to new status they need to feel that other key people also acknowledge this change. The funeral service, therefore, is a key event in the total rite of passage.

		Total	Status of bereaved		
			Widow	Widower	Other
Base of percentages	weighted	758	312	125	321
	unweighted	746	313	123	328
Kinds of help specified:		%	%	%	%
Helping to arrange the funeral e.g. seeing the undertakers, contacting relatives, providing refreshments		57	57	58	56
Accompanying the bereaved when contacting officials or making funeral arrangements		35	32	41	35
Contacting 'officials' e.g. seeing the registrar or coroner, notifying insurance company or employer of deceased, sorting out deceased's affairs		33	43	25	27
Providing comfort or moral support e.g. staying with the bereaved, looking after the bereaved or his/her children		15	19	21	8
Sorting through and disposing of deceased's possessions		4	0	8	6
Giving advice to bereaved		3	3	2	9

Table 2. Ways in which family and friends helped the bereaved after the death, analysed by status of the bereaved [24]

The funeral service

Meanwhile our eyes are fixed, not on the things that are seen, but on the things that are unseen: for what is seen passes away; what is unseen is eternal.[25]

During the course of the funeral rites our eyes are to be turned away from the physical remains towards the things 'that are unseen'. Away from who we are, and what we have done in life, to what God in his love has done for us through his Son, Jesus Christ. The service can direct us to the spiritual resources which can aid and encourage us to make the transition from the past to a future in which we must live the rest of our life.

The funeral is an event for all of us. In addition to speaking to the next of kin the funeral should also speak to those others present who may have experienced loss previously, or who may have been put in mind of possible future loss. Attending a funeral in whatever capacity can confront us with the fact that one day we shall die and all this will be happening for us. In that many people do not wish to be reminded of their own mortality they may not wish to be challenged in this way by the service and so may express the preference for a 'short simple service' at the crematorium where they may wish to be cushioned from facing the finality of physical separation by death.

If the funeral ritual is to be effective in facilitating the grief of the bereaved then those present must be actively involved. This may be by joining in with the responses, the saying of the psalms together, one of the group reading a lesson, singing a hymn, as well as the non-verbal ways of touching and holding each other and passing tissues. Apart from the clergy and the funeral directors most people are not familiar with the various funeral services of the different churches and so need careful direction so that they can be caught up in the ritual without becoming anxious about whether they should be standing, sitting or kneeling.

Apart from the planning of the service (preferably with the family prior to the funeral) and their own personal preparation, ministers have the key function of actually conducting it. They are invested with authority and looked to for leadership in seeing that the 'ritual is effective' and that 'Bert has a good send off'. It can be a daunting task to be faced with a varied group of distressed people, about whom one may know very little, and to try and unite them into a meaningful act of worship within the space of a few minutes.

As pastors lead their congregations in prayer and worship and exhortation, they renew and re-symbolize their ability to be representative persons bearing the wisdom, resources, and authority of Christian faith. No other helping profession in our society possesses a ready way to exhibit ritually its representation of a distinct tradition of helping.[26]

The minister must endeavour to speak clearly and confidently, to look people in the eye, and to be seen to be calmly in control of what happens. If we are to be able to proclaim the word and love of God in and through the service then we must be calm, confident and yet remain sensitive to what the people are feeling and may wish to express. David Shepherd described this ability as *expressive leadership* by 'the person who can put into words the strong feelings of the group . . .'[27] The minister is, therefore, looked to as someone who is able to draw together the many emotions experienced by the people present and to offer them up as part of a true act of worship.

Many bereaved people are frightened by the intensity of their feelings, and the presence of other people whom they trust, coupled with a sensitive and calm leadership of the ritual, can enable them to feel safe about expressing feelings at the funeral. The funeral is something that mourners may dread in anticipation because of the finality of the physical separation which it rightly expresses. However, it is important to have a public recognition of the fact of death and to provide for the reverent disposal of the body. The Christian service also clearly proclaims God's love at the time of death and separation, commends the deceased to God's grace and care, and makes plain the eternal unity of Christian people (living and departed) within the risen Body of our Lord Jesus Christ. This is sometimes made difficult by the confusion between re-vivification and resurrection. Some people find it hard to distinguish between these two and feel that the Church has not always made it clear.[28]

When it is possible to set the funeral service in the context of the Holy Communion it becomes very clear that the prime task is to share in an act of worship rather than the ritual disposal of a body, important though that is. Sometimes this will take place as a requiem coinciding with the reception of the body into church the night before the actual funeral. On other occasions the funeral service and Eucharist will combine as the main church service prior to the committal of the body by burial or cremation. The eucharistic setting focuses our attention on Christ's sacrifice on the cross, our assurance of future resurrection, and reminds us clearly of the communion of saints. It also serves to emphasize that the funeral is not a private event and that others of the congregation may also be experiencing loss through the death of one of their members and may wish to be part of the communion and thanksgiving.

The sermon While the words used and the framework of the liturgy are important to the effectiveness of the funeral rite, the sermon presents both a challenge and an opportunity to guide people towards a healthy resolution of their grief, and to refer to the transition that is taking place.

Historically there has been a reluctance to say too much about the deceased at the funeral, and the Church of England Prayer Book makes no provision for a sermon. In the new Alternative Service Book the sermon is optional. This is not a time for an exposition of the psychology of grief. However, there is a need to acknowledge the sense of loss and, where they are known to the minister, to reflect some of the emotions represented in those attending. It is usually possible to include a note of thanksgiving and the pre-funeral visit will have given an opportunity to find out about the deceased, and the feelings that others had about him or her. Even when there is ambivalence in the various relationships it should be possible to find aspects of the person for which to give thanks, and to make some offering of the 'loose ends' of a person's life and the mourners connected with them.

What is said about the deceased, about the reality and certainty of death, and the feelings and reactions of the bereaved, all needs to be set against the Christian teaching on death and resurrection and the belief in the ultimate union of all believers in Christ. Eulogy and sentimentality can detract from the basic Christian message.

The approach to the sermon will depend upon the circumstances surrounding the death, what we have gleaned about the family, and our own attitude towards death and the extent to which we personally have come to terms with it. It is hard to preach with confidence about something which causes us great anxiety. If this is the case it will be tempting to hide behind platitudes and thus be unable to convey conviction in what we are saying.

In preparing the sermon or address caution may be required, especially if not everyone present knows the circumstances of the death. It is advisable to check with the family before revealing, e.g. that the deceased was HIV positive and died of AIDS. The arrival of HIV/AIDS in our community has been very influential in helping society face the reality of death and bereavement. Many people who are HIV positive as well as those who have gone on to develop AIDS, and those who care for them, have been very courageous in sharing their reactions to their disease and approaching death. Many would be quite willing for the funeral address to refer to the reality of the situation, but others may feel that some family members are not ready to be so open. Discussion with the significant people in the deceased's life can usually clarify what would be appropriate. Such discussion is important if the address is not to be too bland to 'speak' to anyone attending the funeral.

We must learn the art of being aware and understanding what another is feeling – the anger, the doubts, the guilt, the fears for the future. In fact all the normal grief reactions described earlier. Because of the strength of some of these feelings, the distressed mourner's attention may wander and only pick up the occasional sentence here and there. Therefore, one cannot develop involved theological arguments, but needs to use simple and straightforward statements. What is said and heard can go deep and stick for years in the minds of the mourners – for good and ill. As one lady said some years later, 'I don't remember much about what he said, but I could tell that he meant it.'

One difficulty, if we accept the thesis that the funeral can be an important rite of passage, is the tendency to reduce or to shorten the whole proceedings on the grounds that it is unnecessary suffering. There is also clearly a difference between the funeral of a faithful parishioner and the funeral of an unknown person conducted by the minister 'on duty' at the crematorium.

In the case of the funeral of someone we know nothing about prior to the arrival of the family at the burial chapel or crematorium, it is important to find some way of meeting the family before commencing the service proper. This can either be done in the chapel before starting the service, or by going out to the first car and introducing yourself to the chief mourners and making some personal contact. In this way you may at least find out what relationship they have to the deceased and you are expressing a concern to relate to them personally, rather than formally commencing the sentences and marching into the chapel. The funeral director can usually give you some information as to the manner of death: suicide, cot death, sudden coronary, or long-standing illness. Although there can sometimes be a desire not to hang about but to get on with the service, the five minutes or so that the above may take tells the family you wish it to be *their* service and that you appreciate it is their only one, even if it is your fifth as the 'duty minister'.

It can occasionally happen that the 'duty minister' at the crematorium may be asked if he or she is willing to conduct a funeral service, for example for a Hindu or Sikh since there is no Hindu priest available. From the point of view of the family the Christian minister would be acceptable because he or she is to be revered as a 'holy person'. One can either refuse to take the service, or explain that as a Christian minister one would have to take a Christian service, or conduct the service and refer only to God. Time should be spent before the service commences to ensure that there is mutual respect for each other's beliefs and understanding about what is being said in the service.[29]

The funeral of an elderly person with no relatives or friends to mourn the loss can be a sad occasion. If the deceased person's estate cannot pay for a funeral this may lead to what is often described as a 'pauper' or 'contract' funeral in a marginal grave, paid for by the health authority or the local authority. The funeral is usually held in the early morning with the 'duty minister' and funeral director the only people present. Rather than a brief committal at the graveside, if we accept that each human being is special in the sight of God, then there should be a decent funeral service to mark the end of that life. If the person has died in hospital and has been a long-stay patient the hospital chaplain can enquire whether some of the staff or fellow patients may wish to attend. One of the authors previously worked at a hospital where the fellow residents in a unit for the mentally handicapped would go by mini-bus to attend the funeral of one of their 'unit family'. In spite of their handicap they too had grief to express.

What if there is no body? We mentioned earlier that it is important to have a public recognition of the fact of death and this is especially important when there is no body to grieve over. The deceased may have been 'lost at sea' or have died in an explosion, or in the case of an early miscarriage or abortion there may be no body to bury, but still a death to grieve for.

It may be that the body has been donated to a medical school for the purposes of anatomy. If this happens one condition is that the remains be decently disposed of, with an appropriate service, in accordance with the expressed wishes of the deceased. This usually takes place about two years later and the relatives can say whether they wish to be notified and to attend at the committal.

In all cases where there is no body to dispose of it is advisable that there should be some ritual to mark personally and socially what has happened. A memorial service or a requiem is often the right way to proclaim publicly the fact of the death and to enable separation and transition to take place. Failure to do something at this time may leave the bereaved very unsure and anxious about how and where to express what they are feeling. Grief may then be postponed and this can be the prelude for abnormal grieving patterns subsequently. If the bereaved is a patient in hospital at the time of the funeral it can be beneficial if the hospital chaplain visits to see whether the patient would like prayers, a service, or simply some company at the time of the funeral.

Many medical schools which benefit from the donation of bodies for anatomy hold an annual memorial service, to which relatives of those who have donated their bodies are invited. These services are usually very well attended and clearly fulfil a need. They also represent a public acknowledgement by the medical school of the donor's generosity but also of the relatives' generosity for letting this gift go through and coping with the inevitable delay before the body is finally 'laid to rest'.

Death of pets Clergy may sometimes be asked if they can help with an appropriate ritual to say goodbye to a pet. There is little doubt that people can form very strong relationships with their pets. When the pet dies these affectionate bonds are broken and the pet's carer can have a marked grief reaction. They may find it very difficult to leave their pet with a vet to be disposed of and may feel they want some form of ceremony. Evelyn Waugh's novel *The Loved One* addressed this need in a fictional sense from a USA perspective. However, a growing need in this country has led to the development of pet cemeteries and crematoria where people can take their pet and arrange a suitable funeral. It is for individual clergy to decide whether or not it is appropriate for them to participate in such ceremonies.

The Funeral Ombudsman At the time of a funeral the relatives of the deceased can become very distressed if the events around the time of the death and the funeral do not seem respectful to the person who has died. Sometimes grief will create a dissatisfaction which may result in anger being displaced onto the family doctor, the hospital, minister or funeral director. However, if they have real grounds for complaint, the Funeral Ombudsman Scheme[30] can be helpful. The complainant can ask the Ombudsman to investigate, adjudicate and, if appropriate, award compensation. The main area of complaint is the presentation of the deceased when relatives go to view the body. Other common causes of complaint relate to cremation and issues around the disposal or actual loss of ashes.

In bereavement there is not only an external social change of status, but also an internal change which is initiated by the grief process. In the funeral ritual the next of kin is assured that he or she will live on without the deceased. The separation is represented as a completed one and the survivors are encouraged to make the transition to their new social identity leading to incorporation back into the community.

Incorporation

This third part of the rite of passage aids the re-entry into the community of those who have been branded or stigmatized by death.[31] In that the funeral encapsulates the entire rite of passage, in miniature, then such re-entry can be symbolized by the return to the house of family and friends following the funeral. People usually return to the house for an act of group sharing. It is a time for offering support to the next of kin, for reminiscence, renewing old acquaintances and perhaps for settling old scores. Traditionally there is a meal and drinks. A great deal of emotion is expressed as laughter or tears, and on occasions it can lead to a riotous party. Such gatherings are more common in the north of Britain than in the south.

> The wake itself signifies a return to chaos, a release from the restraints of normal 'good behaviour' and propriety, a real cultural disintegration, analogous to the dissolution of the deceased's earthly identity and authority. The final requiem and burial are thus islanded in time, and attain a kind of post-cathartic solemnity, the deliberation of grief is acknowledged and accepted, the calm of all passion spent. Such post-liminal rites act as monuments to whatever has gone before; not only the death of people or animals, but of institutions, epochs, stages of growth, even attitudes of mind. They are real 'rites of passage'.[32]

In some parts of Britain it is also the practice for the family to attend their local church on the Sunday following the funeral and for the deceased and family to be referred to during the course of the service. This helps to symbolize the ongoing concern for the bereaved by the local Christian congregation.

Active support for the bereaved may not continue for very long. The family may need to return home to various parts of the country, the neighbours need to return to the needs of work and their own families. People also get tired of hearing what 'a marvellous husband' Harry was. Sometimes it is the bereaved who withdraw from the community. In the early days following the death the next of kin may be very open about their personal life and financial affairs with other people. Later they may wish that they had not talked so freely with some people and so may withdraw and, in effect, say to others 'keep out'. This often causes hurt and if other people do not understand they stop visiting and make such comments as, 'Fancy not letting me in, after all I've done for her.'

If the bereaved go away to stay with relatives immediately after the funeral this can delay or complicate *incorporation*. By going away at this stage the community does not have the easy opportunity to visit. When the bereaved returns home weeks later the community has returned to its normal activities and the opportunity and stimulus has been lost for visiting and support. This can lead to a heightening of the isolation that the bereaved will experience anyway.

Full incorporation of the bereaved back into the community is parallel to the final phase of grief which we described earlier as *'resolution'*.[33] We are, therefore, thinking in terms of a period of time nearer to 18 months than the two or three months that people usually allow. Attempts to hurry the grief process are often an expression of *our* anxiety and embarrassment in the face of grief. A difficulty that faces many people in our own society is the lack of a structure within which to do their grief work, and which would mark off the end of grief.

Within the Jewish community, for example, there is a clear structure which is designed to aid the expression of grief. After the burial the community turns its attention to the next of kin, and on the return from the cemetery a meal will have been prepared as an expression of their care and the period of consolation begins. First there are three days for deep grief. The remainder of the first seven days (*Shiva*) of mourning are for condolence calls to be made, the visitor's main role being to listen not to talk, and to prepare food for the mourner. The remainder of this initial period of 30 days is for gradual adjustment known as *Shaloshim*, during which the mourner may return to work but lives a restricted life. The full period of mourning for a parent is one year from the date of the death, and so the remaining 11 months are for remembrance and healing until *Jahrzeit* (anniversary).[34] A tombstone may be erected and consecrated during this period and at *Jahrzeit* the *Kaddish* is recited in the synagogue and a memorial candle is lit. At the end of the year it is expected that the mourner will be well integrated back into the life of the community. Not all members of the community will adhere equally strictly to this pattern, however.

In the absence of such a structure the bereaved look to various key people in the community for guidance as to whether certain actions are deemed acceptable or unacceptable and when grief may be officially 'ended' in the sense that it is all right to socialize. A young widow who wishes to remarry may seek approval from the local community in case she is censured later for marrying 'before her first is cold in t'grave'. One key person is the minister and this serves to underline the importance of post-funeral visits.

The post-funeral visit

In a busy pastoral area, with many funerals, one may argue that there is little time for a minister to make all the post-funeral visits that they might like to make. However, because of their special role in society, the minister, as well as being the person who conducted the funeral, is often the only person who can make an uninvited call on the bereaved. Perhaps one reason for not making such calls is related more to uncertainty about the purpose of such visits rather than lack of time. If we are unsure about what to say or do then it is not difficult to find reasons to postpone a visit.

Unlike the pre-funeral visit, where there may be a clear agenda and lots of other people around, after the funeral the minister is more likely to find the bereaved on their own. By this time the person will be less shocked and many of the feelings of grief may be under the surface waiting for an opportunity to be expressed. Since many people like to put on a good face for the minister we may gain the impression that all is well and that there is no need to rush back. One of the prime purposes of this visit, and any subsequent calls, is to provide an opportunity for the expression of grief if the person wishes to. If the minister is prepared to listen in an accepting way the bereaved will sometimes feel that it is safe to express, for example, some of the ambivalent feelings about the deceased and about God.

While exaggeration of grief feelings may be fairly obvious, one should also take note of stoicism, which can be equally unhelpful. Some Christians feel that grief is inappropriate for them and that they should be happy that their loved one is with God. This may lead to their exhibiting stoical indifference in the face of death and reassuring the minister that they are 'content and happy'. Here the person is saying what he or she thinks the minister wants to hear, a sort of 'baptized stoicism'. This response to loss often leads to delay or postponement of grief until the person feels they have permission to grieve and that it is not exhibiting lack of faith in God.

If the minister can talk about how normal, though distressing, a thing grief is, this can often give reassurance where the bereaved may secretly have felt very worried about their reactions. A reference to the way in which Jesus expressed grief when his friend Lazarus died[35] may also help the person to feel safe in expressing some of their feelings.

> We have not incurred any grievous sin by our tears. Not all weeping proceeds from unbelief or weakness. Natural grief is one thing, distrustful sadness is another . . .[36]

The bereaved may also find it difficult to pray and to realize the presence of Christ with them in their grief. This can be a time to assure them that others are praying for them in spite of their feeling that God is absent. .

> Meanwhile, where is God? This is one of the most disquieting symptoms. When you are happy, so happy that you have no sense of needing Him, so happy that you are tempted to feel His claims upon you as an interruption, if you remember yourself and turn to Him with gratitude and praise, you will be – or so it feels – welcomed with open arms. But go to Him when your need is desperate, when all other help is vain, and what do you find? A door slammed in your face, and a sound of bolting and double bolting on the inside. After that silence . . .[37]

Another function of the post-funeral visit can be to aid the bereaved in freeing themselves from painful associations. For example, the widow whose husband was a member of the church choir may find she cannot face going to church for a while because she keeps seeing the gap where her husband used to be. The minister's visit to the home may help the widow to feel that until she is ready to go to church, then the church will come to her.

The church, of course, is more than the minister, and many congregations may be able to share in the post-funeral visits. Some ministers keep a card-index file so that they can ensure that they make a visit near to the time of the anniversary. We do not wish to advocate 'professional neighbourliness', but if a Christian congregation is to be actively involved in such visiting they need to be prepared and supported.

The sort of preparation envisaged is that which should be a normal part of our ministry to the congregation, namely helping people to focus upon death in the context of the resurrection. At any one moment the congregation will contain people who are preparing to face *future* grief and people who are working through *past* grief. The main difficulty for many people, which makes visiting the bereaved difficult, is their own anxieties about death and dying.

The Christian congregation should be one group in society whose members are willing and able to share the pain of loss experienced by others. This should partly be because their faith and instruction enables them to overcome the fear of death, and partly because they have the backing of a supportive and prayerful group. Where such pastoral visits by the local congregation are feasible the visitor can refer appropriate people to the minister. They will also be expressing in a practical way that the church cares and thus be enabling the gradual incorporation of the bereaved back into the community.

There are other groups who can offer support in various ways to the bereaved: *The Compassionate Friends*, for parents who have lost a child; *Cruse*, for widows and widowers and other members of the family; and the *Stillbirth and Neonatal Death Society*.[38] These and other self-help groups are made up of people who have experienced similar types of loss, and have been able to complete their grief work in a healthy manner. These groups usually have professional advisers who can offer support, expert advice and training as required.

Post-funeral visits may not be easy but they offer great pastoral opportunities. However, one of the biggest sins that can be committed by the minister, or any other visitor to the bereaved, is that of promising to visit and then never making that visit. Nahum Tate recognized this temptation when he wrote:

Take the bowsey short leave of your nymphs on the shore,
 And silence their mourning
 With vows of returning,
Though never intending to visit them more.[39]

Headstones and memorials

Because of the difficulty of letting go, and the wish to have a tangible reminder of the deceased, a suitably inscribed headstone or plaque is usually erected on the grave or other suitable place. Some of our forebears erected very elaborate tombstones. It is difficult to know whether the size was in proportion to the real (or imagined) importance of the deceased, or to ensure that the deceased stayed where they were!

Many church authorities have clear instructions about headstones to discourage ostentation as well as to aid the upkeep of the churchyard. An alternative way for many people to commemorate and 'immortalize' the deceased is to give a gift in memory to the church, or some other institution such as a research body connected with the cause of the person's death. Gifts to the church should be 'to the glory of God' first and in memory of the deceased second. Problems can sometimes occur if the bereaved give a gift without prior consultation. Refusal of an inappropriate gift is often seen as a slight against the deceased.

It is important that the mortal remains of a baptized Christian should be decently laid to rest and therefore the cremated remains should be interred and not scattered in some inappropriate place like a golf course or cricket pitch. The interment of ashes often occurs later with appropriate ritual and prayers in either a specially appointed churchyard or crematorium garden of remembrance. Care should be taken to manage the interment so as not to cause distress to relatives by ash blowing on them. Where possible the ashes should be interred in the casket.

Prayers for the dead

One of the purposes of ritual is to reduce anxiety, and the anxiety about what has happened to the deceased has influenced aspects of the religious ritual throughout the history of the Church.

In the early days of the Church this anxiety led to the practice of baptism of the dead. This practice later disappeared and gave way to prayers for the dead. St Augustine was then influential in shaping much of the thought on this topic when he stated that intercessory prayer could do more to increase God's mercy than any pompous funeral or huge commemorative stone which (while comforting the living) was of no avail to the dead. It was out of such intercessory prayer, together with Holy Communion at the graveside, that the Mass for the Dead grew. Coupled to this was the development of the doctrine of purgatory and the growth of the chantry system[40] with all the attendant abuses. The Reformation sought to change all this and, as a result, praying for the dead has been a controversial subject for many ever since.

Within the Church of England, the Doctrinal Commission sought to resolve the conflicts by producing, in 1970, a report entitled *Prayer and the Departed*.[41] This document, with the ensuing debate, was important in the formulation of the funeral service in the Alternative Service Book (ASB) of the Church of England.

Those who disagree with petition for the dead argue that such prayers are unnecessary for someone who is already 'in Christ' for he or she is already enjoying rest and peace in Christ. They would further argue that to pray for non-Christians is wrong because it is in this life that they should make their decision about Christ. Otherwise one could put off making one's decision until after death when either 'the light is turned out' or you know for sure that the gospel is true. Praying for the dead, it is further argued, undermines the Christian assurance of being in Christ since it implies that something may be lacking which needs fulfilling after death.

Those who support petition for the dead claim that if we believe in the communion of saints then we should continue to pray for those we love who have passed to a new mode of existence. Similarly there is no reason why we should not ask them to pray for us. If, instead of dying, they had gone to live in Manchester, we would not hesitate to contact them and ask them to pray for some particular need. We would also pray for them as they commenced their new life in Manchester. In praying for the dead one is not asking God to change his mind about the person for, after all, he knows them better than we do. Rather we are expressing our faith and trust in God's loving mercy to 'grant that your servant may know the fulness of life which you have promised to those who love you.'[42] A further point made by those who support prayers for the dead is that if we are not undermining the doctrine of justification by faith when we pray for someone who is alive, why should we be implying a denial of that doctrine if we pray for them after death?

Whatever our personal doctrinal position regarding prayers for the dead, many of the relatives we meet following a death are looking for reassurance and an easing of their anxiety about what has happened to the person who has died. The commendation of the departed to the loving mercy of God, an act of thanksgiving for the life shared, the belief in the resurrection and the hope of meeting again, represent areas of agreement for many. This agreement is well expressed at the end of the funeral service of the Church of England:[43]

> May God in his infinite love and mercy bring the whole Church, living and departed in the Lord Jesus, to a joyful resurrection and the fulfilment of his eternal kingdom. Amen.

Before offering any prayer at the time of death, therefore, the minister needs to spend a little time picking up the feelings that are around in the family regarding both the deceased and God. This reflects what was said earlier that if a ritual is to be seen as relevant it must be in tune with needs at the psychological, theological and sociological levels.[44] This sensitive 'picking up of the atmosphere' will enable the minister to formulate a prayer or prayers which express the reality of what is being experienced. Therefore, rather than picking up a book to say what we always say on such occasions, we must try to find out what *they* wish to be said. Such prayer, therefore, will usually include an act of thanksgiving, a commendation of the dead person, a reaffirmation of the Christian assurance that we are united in Christ from whom nothing can separate us,[45] our hope for future resurrection, and a request that God will grant to those who mourn strength and courage to face the future.

The mixed feelings which take place in certain relationships may also be reflected in these prayers when it seems right to do so. Sometimes one has the impression that by the use of *'requiescat in pace'* the family are implying the wish that the dead stay where they are and do not return!

The Holy Communion and the Requiem represent a unique meeting point between God and man, between the living and the departed. For those who believe in the sacramental presence of Christ in the consecrated bread and wine, they can also feel very close to the faithful departed (who are in Christ) when they go forward to receive Communion. It is for this reason that many find that, apart from their normal regular attendance at Communion, a special annual occasion, such as All Souls' Day on 2 November, can be especially significant and reassuring regarding *incorporation* for the deceased.

Children and funerals

A child's attitude to death will be coloured by our own and if we are not able to face the fact of death they will find it difficult also. To tell the child that 'Mummy is in hospital', when in fact Mummy is dead, can lead to a multitude of problems later. The distrust of the adult by the child, the fear of hospitals and the idea that any separation might lead to death can all result from this avoidance. It does not help to shut a child out of the grief that a whole family shares since this does not give them an opportunity and structure within which to express their grief.

Research has shown that certain groups of bereaved children are more likely to develop subsequent psychiatric disorders later in life than others. The children at most risk are those bereaved of a parent between the ages of three and five, or in early adolescence.[46] In view of what has been said about the possible efficacy of ritual in the grief process, should a child attend a funeral of a close relative? One cannot be dogmatic and say that all should or should not attend a funeral, since it depends on who has died, the age of the child, the attitudes of the family and the form of service to be used.

It is important, above all things, to try to find out what the *child* wishes to do and not to be overprotective. However, in encouraging the child to talk we must also beware of the temptation to rush the pace. It is difficult for a child to make a decision without knowing what they are likely *to see* and be involved in. Therefore we should try to explain the funeral service and what the coffin will be like. All of us have our own way of explaining things to our children and we often use our own language. One mother explained to her daughter that just as you have a special casket for precious jewellery, so a coffin is like a special casket to hold something very precious – the body of the person who has died.

Where the committal is to be preceded by a service in church it may be decided that the child attends the church service and then returns home with a member of the family while the others go to the graveside or crematorium. Some children may wish to attend the entire ceremony, while others may decide to go and stay with someone until it is all over. One ten-year-old who attended the funeral service in church of a close relative sobbed afterwards and then said, 'Oh, I'm glad I came.' Whatever is decided, it seems important that the child should have a say in the decision and an opportunity to express his or her own feelings about what is happening. Then the child's choice should be accepted as right by the family, without judgemental comment.

Children have a lot of life to live, so it is important to guide them in such a way that they develop wise and healthful attitudes toward their feelings, their lives, and their deaths.[47]

Woodland burials and natural death issues

A growing number of people in our society wish to explore alternative forms of funeral, and therefore have more control over their burial. In particular there has been a growth in requests for 'green' funerals, arranged either by recognized funeral directors or by the family themselves. The ceremony can be conducted by clergy or other faith leaders, members of the British Humanist Association authorized to conduct funerals, or those concerned with woodland burial sites in various parts of the country. Details of help available are gathered usefully in the *New Natural Death Handbook*.[48] There are four main options open to people:

1 *Woodland burial.* This means burial in a woodland site set aside specifically and dedicated to that use. Each plot is subsequently returned to meadow with a tree planted on the grave plot. The coffin must be biodegradable, as must the shroud, or alternatively a wicker basket may be used. All requirements can be purchased privately and prepared by the family alone or with help from funeral directors.
2 *Burial on private land*: for example, in the grounds of one's own home. While this is possible there must be compliance with public health measures, plus consideration of the future use of that land in the event of the death of the

owner or the sale of the property – the value of which can be reduced as that portion *cannot* be sold with the house. 'Subject to any restrictive covenants affecting the use of the land, a place of burial may be established by any person without statutory authority, in private land, provided that no statutory or other "nuisance" such as smell or pollution is caused.'[49] A Certificate of Lawfulness should be applied for from the local authority in order to check if there is likely to be any objection. In addition, legal advice should be sought in respect of any restrictive covenants in the Deeds of the property. Details must go to the Land Burial Register within four days.

3 *Burial at sea.* In theory this is attractive to some people; it seems to require only a free licence in England and Wales from the Ministry of Agriculture, Fisheries and Food (MAFF) and then a boat to take the coffin out into the sea. In practice, however, it is more difficult and costly because of restrictions as to *where* you can perform this, because of trawling. There is also a need to weight the coffin properly to prevent it floating subsequently. Advice is obtainable from the Marine Environmental Protection at the MAFF.

4 *Do It Yourself:* utilizing a local cemetery or crematorium. It is now possible to purchase all you require to arrange a burial or cremation oneself without involving commercial firms. Some practical issues need to be thought about, however. There are legal requirements regarding the certification of death, including in some situations liaison with the coroner. Keeping the dead body at home can also present problems at some times of the year and you may need assistance with refrigeration. Purchasing the coffin and other accessories is not difficult, but it should be realized that not every estate car will take a coffin, unless the car is extra long.

What many people seem to be saying in exploring the above options is that prior to death they may have specific views or needs regarding their own funeral. The family may agree to these and wish to have more control. Many funeral directors are reviewing the service they offer and will assist the family in providing for a more 'green' funeral in keeping with the deceased's wishes and involving the family. It may be possible, for instance, to place personal items in the coffin, or grave, which may range from sealed letters to items of significance to the deceased. At the time of the funeral some families provide boxes at the entrance to the church or crematorium into which people can place items to celebrate the person's life in cards, thoughts, objects reminding people of events, etc. These can then be taken home as part of the memorialization.

Complete DIY funerals do require some reflection on the emotional cost to the family. A sudden, traumatic death can make DIY difficult to achieve because of time-scale, coroner involvement, and especially the deep grief reaction of those who are trying to make the arrangements.

In some cases what the family feel is 'right and appropriate' may be very different from the views of the person who has died. The funeral is a public event to enable others to witness the decent disposal of the dead body, usually according to the custom and practice of the local area. The funeral will therefore also be attended by friends, workmates, people from the local pub, customers who came into the shop, etc. They too will have expectations of what is appropriate, and these might be at variance with those of the family. In some cases these other friends may seem to have known a very different person from the person known to family. Such clashes can leave all involved feeling the funeral was not for them. Advance funeral directives are helpful, whatever the arrangements are, but they should be shared with key family members and executors while the person is alive and well, so that any difficulties can be addressed in advance. Such arrangements may include the involvement of ministers of religion or members of the National Secular Society for non-religious ceremonies. In any case a flexibility in approach should enable a helpful and personalized service or ceremony to be prepared.

Conclusion

We have looked at ways in which ritual does not replace the grief process but can, if used effectively, enable it to happen. In that people in a crisis usually benefit from having a structure within which they may safely express very powerful feelings, the desire to reduce ritual to a minimum is not something necessarily to be welcomed. If we dispense with ritual we may leave people with a further sense of loss: not only have they lost a person through death, but they have also lost a means of coping with that loss. In a review of six bizarre cases[50] where the next of kin kept the dead person in their home and did not arrange for burial, it was found to be significant that three of these situations arose because the surviving relative failed to initiate the appropriate ritual. Decline in ritual in our society is not the only factor leading to unusual expressions of grief, but it can be an important one.

We are not here advocating a return to the codification of death rituals as developed in Victorian times, as instanced in 'Manners and Rules of Good Society' (*The Widow*, 1887):

> The regulation period for a widow's mourning is two years. Of this period crêpe is worn for one year and nine months. For the first twelve months the dress is entirely covered with crêpe. The remaining nine months it should be trimmed with crêpe heavily so for the first six months and considerably less the remaining three. During the last three months black without crêpe should be worn. After the two years half mourning is prescribed . . . [etc.]

What we wish to assert is that a sensitive and flexible approach to the needs of a particular family should lead to a more relevant and effective ritual which can aid the grieving process. Since an inappropriate and ill-prepared ritual may serve to block the grief process, this places a large measure of responsibility on those who arrange the ritual, as well as those who participate in it.

Notes

1 P. W. Speck, *Loss and Grief in Medicine* (Baillière Tindall, 1978).
2 See Appendix C.
3 A. van Gennep, *The Rites of Passage* (Routledge, 1977).
4 R. Lamerton, *Care of the Dying* (Penguin, 1980).
5 Archbishop Anthony Bloom, a talk to hospital chaplains, quoted by N. Autton in *Care of the Dying* (SPCK, 1966), p. 86.
6 N. Autton, *Watch with the Sick* (SPCK, 1976).
7 See S. R. C. Eucharisticum Mysterium, No. 39: AAS 59 (1967) 562.
8 See literature of Guild of S. Raphael; Church in Wales, 'Services for the Sick', or 'A Pocket Ritual' (post-Vatican II) (Mayhew-McCrimmon) for suggested forms of service.
9 P. W. Speck, 'A Relative Nuisance' in *Religion and Medicine*, 3 (SCM, 1976), p. 37.
10 In the case of the Anglican rite the dying person or intended spouse should contact the hospital chaplain or parish priest. They will then make an application to the Registrar of the Court of Faculties at 1 The Sanctuary, London SW1P 3JT.

When the parties wish to be married by non-Anglican rites, or to have a civil ceremony, a personal application should be made by the intended spouse to the local superintendent registrar. The applicant will be required to produce 'a certificate of a registered medical practitioner showing that the person concerned is seriously ill and is not expected to recover and cannot be moved to a place at which in the normal way the intended marriage can be solemnized, and that THAT PERSON IS ABLE TO AND DOES UNDERSTAND THE NATURE AND PURPORT OF THE MARRIAGE CEREMONY'.

11 John Prickett (ed.), *Death* (Living Faiths series, Lutterworth, 1980).

12 See P. W. Speck, *Being There* (SPCK, 1988).

13 P. W. Speck, *Loss and Grief in Medicine*, chapter 8.

14 *The Removal of Cadaveric Organs for Transplantation – A Code of Practice* (DHSS, 1979).

15 ibid.

16 That is, a fetus born dead after 24 weeks' gestation.

17 DHSS Circular DS 211/75 which comments on HM (72) 4.

18 Hospital chaplains should check the mortuary chapel/viewing room arrangements at their hospital, and the policies dictating how they are used. They should also ensure that these areas are adaptable for use by non-Christians.

19 P. J. Hennessy, *Families, Funerals and Finances* (Research Report No. 6, HMSO, 1980).

20 Romans 8.38–9 (RSV).

21 J. Calhoun, *A Disquisition on Government* (1850).

22 M. Young and P. Wilmott, *Family and Kinship in East London* (Routledge, 1957); J. B. Loudon, 'Kinship and Crisis in South Wales', *British Journal of Sociology*, 4 (1961); G. Gorer, *Death, Grief and Mourning in Contemporary Britain* (Darton, Longman and Todd, 1965).

23 R. Firth, J. Hubert and A. Forge, *Families and their Relatives: Kinship in a Middle Class Sector of London* (Routledge, 1970).

24 Hennessy, op. cit., p. 29, Table 2.10.

25 2 Corinthians 4.18 (NEB).

26 W. A. Clebsch and C. R. Jaekle, *Pastoral Care in Historical Perspective* (Harper and Row, 1967), p. 68.

27 D. Shepherd, *Built as a City* (Hodder and Stoughton, 1974), p. 287.

28 G. W. H. Lampe and D. H. McKinnon, *The Resurrection* (Mowbray, 1966).

29 For details of other funeral rites and key texts employed, see J. Prickett, *Death* (Lutterworth, 1980).

30 Further information can be obtained from the Funeral Ombudsman, 26–28 Bedford Row, London WC1R 4AL (Tel. 0171 430 1112).

31 An individual who is seen as being socially 'abnormal' may be reacted to by others in a variety of ways ranging from rejection to over-hearty acceptance or plain embarrassment. Close contact

with death can lead to social contamination (stigmatization) and therefore the need for some form of cleansing prior to reintegration into society. One example of this process is seen in the healing of the ten lepers who were sent to the priest to be *pronounced* clean in order to rejoin their family and community (Luke 17.14). For further discussion of 'stigma' see E. Goffman, *Stigma* (Penguin, 1968).

32 R. Grainger, *Language of the Rite* (Darton, Longman and Todd, 1974), p. 120.

33 See Table 1 on p. 13.

34 For the death of a child, spouse, brother or sister the period of mourning is reduced to 30 days.

35 John, Chapter 11.

36 St Ambrose, on the death of his brother.

37 C. S. Lewis, *A Grief Observed* (Faber, 1973), p. 9.

38 For the addresses of these and other helping groups, see Appendix B.

39 Nahum Tate, *Dido and Aeneas*, Act III.

40 The benefices maintained to say or sing Mass for the soul of the founder and his friends.

41 *Prayer and the Departed*, Report of the Archbishop's Commission (SPCK, 1971).

42 Alternative Service Book, funeral prayers, section 60.

43 ibid., section 13.

44 See p. 71.

45 Romans 8.39.

46 D. Black, 'The Bereaved Child', *Journal of Child Psychology and Psychiatry*, vol. xix (1978), pp. 287-92.

47 E. Jackson, *The Many Faces of Grief* (SCM, 1978), p. 85.

48 N. Albery, G. Elliot and J. Elliot, *The New Natural Death Handbook* (Rider, 1997).

49 See Scottish Office ruling re. Appeal by Ian Alcock (Scottish Office Ref. P/PPA/GD/342, 25 November 1992) discussed in *The New Natural Death Handbook*, pp. 123-31.

50 A. Gardner and M. Pritchard, 'Mourning, Mummification and Living with the Dead', *British Journal of Psychiatry*, no. 130 (1977), pp. 23-8.

SIX

When Grief Goes Wrong

*Those who mourn may mimic madness
to the observer's eye.*[1]

While a normal grief reaction may, in Freud's words, mimic madness, there are times when the grief process goes wrong and does not progress naturally towards *resolution*. In these instances, rather than mimicking madness it may actually lead to psychiatric illness and the need for professional help.

There are various ways in which grief can 'go wrong' and in this chapter we shall look at some of these ways so that those who are involved pastorally may recognize when an appropriate referral may be needed. Although atypical forms of grief do differ in intensity and duration from the more usual reactions to bereavement already described, they do not differ in kind.

There are no symptoms that are peculiar to pathological grief although it seems reasonable to view extreme expressions of guilt, identification symptoms (hypochondriacal illness), and delay in onset of grief of more than two weeks' duration, as indicators that the reaction to bereavement may take a pathological course.[2]

Delay

Delay is the most common abnormal reaction and the postponement of grief may be a short one, or may be delayed for many years. People who have been involved in a disaster may delay expression of grief because of the need to care for others. The delayed grief may then be expressed many months, or years, later following a relatively minor loss. For example, a young woman whose husband was killed in a car crash delayed her grief because of her concern to care for her young children.

Ten months later she was washing up, after the children had gone to school, and broke a glass which had been part of a wedding present. This led to the expression of a severe grief reaction with her smashing the rest of the glasses and screaming out her rage at the husband who had 'left her'. The situation was controlled by the next-door neighbour who rushed around to see what was happening and called the doctor, and stayed with the young widow.

If a woman suffers a bereavement during pregnancy she may interrupt or delay her mourning, because of her preoccupation with the new life within her. Lewis[3] has shown that this may lead to idealization of the child within her and the child may then be seen as a reincarnation of the dead person. An example of this tendency was given earlier[4] when we discussed the Jenkins family and the mother's feelings about the child she was carrying. Lewis advocates that a 'bereaved woman should be helped to mourn at the time of death and to keep alive the expectation of future mourning once her baby is thriving.'[5]

This advice may perhaps be extended to other instances where postponement of grief may be anticipated. A normal part of grief is a period of total preoccupation with the deceased and thus, if there are other people 'competing' for that mental space, either the others will be neglected or the grief will be postponed. This, therefore, supports the importance of the funeral and the associated events as giving space and permission to the bereaved to opt out of any responsibility for others for a short while and express some of their feelings. It also emphasizes the importance of maximum involvement of the bereaved in the funeral arrangements and anything which can establish the reality of what has happened. It may well be that, following the funeral, they will then suppress the grief but the acknowledgement of the reality of the death should have taken place. It is also important that those who are caring for the bereaved give fresh opportunity for the continuation of mourning, once the factors necessitating delay become less urgent. Failure to do this may mean that the person never restarts their grief work and this may lead to subsequent psychiatric illness in later life. If several people are involved with the family there may need to be some consultation between them to decide who is to be the 'key worker' to avoid confusion.

Denial

Because of the pain of separation some people may seek to avoid it by denying reality. To alleviate the constant awareness of the loss the mourner who is expressing excessive separation anxiety may turn to drugs or alcohol, with the attendant danger of addiction or overdose. A glass of whisky at night may help some people to sleep better, but having your teenage child put you to bed because you are in a drunken stupor is quite different. Similarly at certain times in the bereavement the person may need drug medication to calm down or to help them sleep. The selective and short-term use of sedation is clearly right in some instances but can in itself delay the grief process. Hence one should not resort to drugs automatically because of psychological pain as one may still have that pain to work through at a later date. It is the abuse of alcohol or drugs that causes concern rather than the controlled use of them.

There are various other factors which may lead to delay or denial. It may happen because of a previous psychiatric illness such as a personality disorder. It may be because there is no body to see and to bury and so the reality of the death is difficult to accept. It may be because the death itself is seen as socially unacceptable, such as the suicide by a drug addict which led her father to say, 'I never had a daughter,' and thus there was no one to mourn for. The death of a divorced spouse may lead to a similar reaction in that the divorced partner may feel unable to attend the funeral. Feelings of ambivalence or distress at the death of a former marriage partner may reawaken feelings concerning the divorce. These feelings may all be suppressed if one's current marriage partner, or other members of society, deem such grief inappropriate.

Prolongation

Prolongation of grief can be another common problem in that any aspect of the normal grief process may persist for an excessively long time, resulting in the person becoming 'stuck' in one particular part. For example, denial, anger, guilt or idealization may persist for many years, and loneliness and social isolation often heighten these problems. If a person has become 'stuck' it can sometimes help if someone can spend time taking them back over the events leading up to the death, the death itself, the funeral and the feelings experienced at that time.[6] For some people this may be sufficient to get their grieving under way again. If not then a referral to professional help may be necessary.

After a Boston nightclub fire, E. Lindemann worked with the disaster victims and their families. As a result of this experience he was able to formulate several general classes of normal grief. He was also able to describe some of the distorted reactions that one may see when grief is not satisfactorily resolved:[7]

1 Excessive activity with no sense of loss.
2 Development of symptoms similar to those of the deceased, often with related psychosomatic illness.
3 Alteration in relationships with friends and relatives. All social contacts may be shunned and the person become a recluse, or may need supervision because of giving away large sums of money.
4 Furious hostility against people associated with the death event, leading to letters of complaint and wishing to sue the hospital.
5 Behaviour resembling a schizophrenic pattern with lack of emotional expression, living in a daze, and acting in a 'wooden manner'.
6 Severe depression, with insomnia, guilt and bitter self-reproaches. Because the bereaved may feel the need to punish themselves for what has happened there is always an increased risk of suicide. 'I just want to die and be with him.'

Depression

A clinical depression following a death is frequently accompanied by other unresolved grief reactions, such as guilt and self-blame. A young man, who had a tendency towards depressive illness, became depressed following the death of his baby daughter from an inherited disease. Before he and his wife were able to take up the appointment for genetic counselling he committed suicide. In a note he said that he felt genetically responsible for producing an abnormal child and that his wife would be better off without him. She could then marry a 'normal' man and have a normal family.

We earlier remarked that there is a need for 'society' to give permission to the bereaved to end formal mourning and where this does not happen the person can feel guilty and so unduly prolong mourning. Reassurance about one's responsibility for the death may be needed to allay guilt, as in the case of a 'sudden infant death' where remorse may lead to severe depression and the risk of suicide. The supportive role of groups such as the Foundation for the Study of Infant Deaths can be of vital importance in many such cases.

It is sometimes difficult for the lay person to distinguish between the sadness and 'depressed' periods of normal grief and a clinical depression. One of the main distinguishing features is that these episodes in normal grieving are transient and respond well to warmth and attention from other people. In clinical depression giving time and attention to the depressed person seems to have little effect and the person may seem to be just as low spirited and emotionally flat at the end of the visit as at the beginning. A referral to the general practitioner would then be indicated.

In some instances the person may withdraw into the past and preserve things as they were before the death. The classic example of this was Queen Victoria. She had a strong and dependent attachment to Prince Albert, to the extent that she became very upset if they were ever apart from one another during their married life. Such a dependent relationship, apart from any other factors, would have predisposed her to a severe reaction following his death. This has been well illustrated by the work of Lily Pincus,[8] a psychotherapist whose life's work as a marital therapist was given a new direction when she herself was widowed at the age of 65.

The difference between appropriate sadness and clinical depression may not be obvious for various reasons. Cultural cues and variations may be misread by people whose background and assumptions are different. A hospital chaplain was called to the Accident and Emergency Department to see a young woman whose grandmother had died the previous day in the West Indies. The lady concerned had been brought in to the hospital by the police for emergency treatment since she was seen to be singing hymns, holding up her grandmother's photo and praying aloud! She was at some risk of being labelled as mentally ill but the chaplain was immediately able to make contact with her, to say how sorry he was at her grandmother's death and to read the Bible and pray with her in a language that was familiar to her, though not part of the everyday language of the chaplain! It was clear that she was full of feelings which were readily accessible but which could be labelled as mentally ill rather than seen as a very well-rooted cultural statement of distress.

What might seem to be a request for the minister to perform an exorcism to deal with a haunted person or place may very often be connected with unresolved memories. A lady in her forties sought her minister's help since she had experienced her home as haunted following the death of her mother six months before. In conversation it became clear that the daughter had never managed, in her view, to please her mother adequately and that even looking after her mother in her last illness had not produced the love and acceptance she wanted. The minister did say prayers in the house but they were more to do with the undealt-with 'haunting' thoughts and memories.

Distinction should also be maintained between depression and despair. Some people in bereavement may encounter despair, quite literally the inability to hope, and to have any sense of continuity between the past and the present and the future dislocated. This is not a category of distress which is always fully recognized. The best help is often given by those who will quite simply support and be there.[9] There is a working difference between a person who may spend all their time thinking about their death and someone, say a mother whose child has died, who may say quite simply 'I wish I were dead.' The latter may be taken for a suicidal thought when it is quite simply a statement of distress and despair which needs to be heard.

Projection and identification

Lily Pincus maintains that marriages, and relationships generally, are based on two psychological principles: projection and identification.[10] People respond to bereavement in some measure according to which principle is stronger in their make-up. The couples who base their marital relationship on projection form complementary relationships in which the partners develop distinctly divided roles. In the event of a bereavement such couples seem to cope with the loss of their partner, because they are more secure in their autonomy. 'I feel as if something has been torn away from me; therefore I am now separate and have an individual identity.' After due mourning, such a death of a spouse may become a real time of growth and the survivor is seen to 'take on a new lease of life and to blossom'. If, however, too much of the self was projected on to the now lost partner, and if the projection was rigidly maintained, then the bereaved cannot separate sufficiently from the lost partner to truly bury him or her and pathological mourning may result.

The couples who build their marital relationship on identification and cannot bear to have differences, or to be apart from each other, find it especially hard to cope following a bereavement. This seems to be related to their having little sense of personal worth to help them face the world without their marriage partner and so they become increasingly helpless. 'It is as if something has died within me'; thus separation is not something that sets you free but entails loss of self as well. The person will therefore try to keep things as they were since that enables them to retain a sense of identity. This often shows itself through the setting up of a 'shrine' in the person's room so that it is ready for them to 'return to' at any time. A shrine can also be a way in which the bereaved can attempt to make perfect what in real life was far from perfect. So the mother who is bereaved of her very untidy teenage son may keep his bedroom ready for him to return to, but in a very tidy state and totally unrelated to how it looked when the son was alive. What is bizarre and atypical for one family may not be for another and such behaviour has to be assessed in context.[11] A widower aged 80 who lovingly preserves his wife's dressing table as it always used to be is in a different category from the young mother who turns her dead child's bedroom into a shrine and allows no one to use it.

Identification can also manifest itself in the adoption of personality traits of the deceased and with the illness symptoms of the deceased. This may either show itself as hypochondriasis or with the conviction that one has the same disease that one's spouse died from. In such cases the pain experienced physically is real enough, even though the cause may be psychological, and much reassurance may be needed from the family and the doctor, as well as encouragement to resume the social activities from which they withdrew into illness.

Supportive ministering

The minister of religion who is visiting the bereaved and identifies that grief is going wrong, or is unresolved, may be able to restimulate the grieving process by taking the person back to look at the events and feelings prior to the death and at the time of the death. If this does not lead to any movement forward for the bereaved person then it is necessary to consult with or refer the person for more specialist help. Apart from the general practitioner there are various other people and groups who may be able to help, according to what is available in the locality: health visitors, the community nursing service, social services who offer an emergency 'on call' service in most areas, and the various self-help and befriending groups such as Cruse, Samaritans, Citizens' Advice, counselling centres, Stillbirth Society, etc.[12] Crucial factors in how grief is faced may relate to the relationship with the dead or lost person, the manner of the death or loss and the person's previous experience of earlier losses. It is possible to identify risk factors which tend to predict a poor outcome after bereavement, and Table 3 shows some of these. It must be borne in mind that these factors do not guarantee, but predict, a greater likelihood of a poor outcome.

ANTECEDENT

Relationship with the deceased
   Kinship- Spouse (especially widow)
     Child (especially aged 1–5),
     Twin
     Parent
     Grandparent
   Security of attachment
     Bereaved dependent on deceased
     Deceased overly dependent on bereaved
     Bereaved ambivalent towards deceased

Childhood experiences (especially insecure parenting and losses of significant persons)
Later experiences (especially losses of significant persons)
Previous mental illness (especially depressive illness)
Life crises prior to the bereavement

Mode of death
   Unexpected and untimely deaths
   Inexplicable deaths (e.g. cot deaths)
   Very long terminal illness
   Multiple deaths
   Violent or horrific deaths
   Disenfranchised deaths (i.e. deaths that cannot be acknowledged or mourned)

Culpable deaths (especially murder or manslaughter)
Suicide

CONCURRENT
Young age
Low self-esteem
Personality
    Grief prone
    Inhibition of feelings
Low socio-economic status (social class)

SUBSEQUENT
Family seen as unsupportive
Social isolation
Illness and other emergent stresses
Lack of life opportunities (options closed)

Adapted from C. M. Parkes, *Bereavement: Studies of Grief in Adult Life*, 3rd edn (Penguin, 1996).

Table 3. Risk factors associated with poor outcome after bereavement

If ministers themselves feel supported then they may be able to continue to support the bereaved person for longer and to continue their pastoral caring alongside, and in co-operation with, that offered by other professionals. This can be especially important when the referral has been to a psychiatrist, because of the fear of stigma which the bereaved may have. If the minister makes the referral and then drops out of the picture it may be interpreted by the bereaved that you are glad to have 'dumped' them on to someone else, or that now they are 'psychiatric' you won't want to know them. The *way* in which referral is made is as important as who the referral is made to.

The support of ministers in this aspect of their ministry raises the question of what is the role of the Christian congregation towards the bereaved in their community, and what sort of help and training might they need if they become actively involved in caring for the bereaved and the dying? What opportunities exist for the development of insights and skills in this aspect of pastoral care and who can ministers turn to for help with *their* feelings arising out of this work? In the next chapter we look at the minister in person.

Notes

1 S. Freud, 'Mourning and Melancholia' in *Complete Psychological Works of Sigmund Freud*, vol. xiv (1914–16), (Hogarth).
2 C. M. Parkes, *Bereavement* (Penguin, 1975), p. 142.
3 E. Lewis, 'Inhibition of Mourning by Pregnancy: Psychopathology and Management', *British Medical Journal*, 2 (1979), pp. 27–8.
4 See Chapter 1, p. 4.
5 Lewis, op. cit., p. 27.
6 See Figure 2 on p. 66.
7 E. Lindemann, 'Symptomatology and Management of Acute Grief', *American Journal of Psychiatry*, 101 (1944), p. 141.
8 L. Pincus, *Death and the Family* (Faber, 1976).
9 See the reference to 'spiritual distress' in P. W. Speck, *Being There* (SPCK, 1988), pp. 33–7.
10 *Projection* is the process by which we may interpret events and situations by reading our own experiences and feelings into them. In this way we may attribute our own feelings and motives to other people. *Identification* is the process by which we may unconsciously model our behaviour on that of someone to whom we are emotionally tied. Thus we may either extend our identity *into* someone else, borrow our identity *from* someone else, or fuse our identity *with* someone else. See Pincus (1976) p. 26ff. for further discussion of these concepts.
11 A. Gardner and M. Pritchard, 'Mourning, Mummification and Living with the Dead', *British Journal of Psychiatry* 130 (1977).
12 See Appendix B for details of existing groups.

SEVEN

Focus on the Minister

We have already looked at the customs and processes which may isolate the dying person and those close to them from the rest of the society of which they are part. Communities, however, usually give certain people unspoken permission to break the taboos and come near to the scene of the death. Doctors, nurses, funeral directors and ministers of religion seem to be the four categories of people who are today empowered to deal with the issues which surround death. In addition to these, volunteers increasingly play a key role in the way many specialist palliative care programmes provide for the needs of bereaved people. However, great emphasis needs to be placed on careful recruitment, selection and training if they are to be effective. There also needs to be an effective level of supervision. Experience at many in-patient units shows that this is not free of cost, as there needs to be a regular intake of new volunteers who require training. However, they do help to underline the normality of grief and avoid any tendency to pathologize grief.[1]

In this chapter we will try to examine how ministers of religion may become more aware of their own needs in order to offer more effective help to others. John Hinton[2] says, 'The priest has for some people an essential part to play in preparing a person for death . . . There is much to be said for a doctor or someone who knows of the patient's fatal illness inquiring after his religious views so that "the minister can give continued help to the patient and his family so long as it is needed".' (The current *New Dictionary of Medical Ethics* has several references to the importance of spiritual care in medicine, especially in relation to palliative care. Similarly in the *Oxford Textbook of Palliative Medicine* spiritual care features and there are many references to the role of clergy and chaplains.[3]) Most clergy will know from experience that their duties are expected to involve visiting sick people at home or in hospital. They will bring with them, even before they speak, a series of complicated expectations, both their own and those of the person they are visiting, and much will depend on how aware they are of these expectations.

What does the minister represent?

The minister visiting a sick person has a function which in some respects is different from that of others. The Ordination Service of the Church of England, paralleled in other ordinals and commissioning services, makes it quite clear that ministers are expected to visit sick people, not on the basis of their sickness but of their humanity.[4] A person's illness may affect considerably the context of the visit and will involve the sensitivities of the minister in a particular way, but it does not of itself provide a reason for visiting. Ministers may often be tempted to ask a *diagnostic* sort of question, such as 'What is wrong with you?' Or they may be tempted to try to connect, often with the sick person's apparent connivance, the current crisis with something which has happened in the past, and try to answer the question, 'What have I done?' – which is a *moralistic* question. The question is, however, pastorally developed quite differently in the Book of Genesis[5] when God asks of the Adam or the Man, when they have lost sight of each other, '*Where* are you?' That is not, of course, offered as a crude pastoral technique but it remains a crucial question for the minister.

It has been the experience of the authors, as hospital chaplains, that in a crisis such as serious illness or bereavement the function which the minister of religion may fulfil at the first encounter may quite simply be that of a 'walking, talking visual-aid' or 'ikon'. What they say may be much less important than what they are perceived to represent. One article[6] speaks of the clergy as 'carriers of other people's longings', by which we mean that those who have consciously abandoned religious practice, even sometimes any sort of personal God, may have expectations of the clergy, almost as if the clergy have sometimes to represent for others beliefs which they may or may not consciously hold. Ministers may find themselves caught in complicated situations where their representative function demands that they speak with some sort of confidence, and where there is little space for private feelings and beliefs.

It is one thing for a man to face up to the doubts in his own mind and the changes that are occurring around him. It is quite another thing to expect this man to confront the world as though he were perfectly confident in his views – especially if we are asking him to demonstrate his total and reassuring command in situations which tend to bring out feelings of anguish and impotence in most of us. The minister, in short, may be expected to say and do precisely the right thing in the death situation because he is really 'in the know'.[7]

So a considerable investment may be held, even by those who have no formal religious belief, in the representative role of the minister in terms of unchangingness and security. But his ability to behave, and sometimes to say things which may sensitively challenge the established expectations may also be crucial. A hospital chaplain has told of sitting by the bed of a small baby who was dying of a chronic disorder, without speaking for a period of about ten minutes, and then, in response to a challenging question from the parents as to why this had been allowed to happen, saying quietly, 'I don't know.' He felt that he should have been able to say something rather more useful to the relatives but received a postcard from them two or three weeks after the child's death which said quite simply, 'Thank you for all the helpful things you said.' The resources of prayer and the sacraments, and sometimes the silent presence of the minister, often give structure and space to the expression of mixed feelings, such as hope and despair, joy and pain, faith and doubt.

The pastoral care which the minister gives is not, of course, something given by 'experts' to non-experts. The dying have much to teach those who care for them that is necessary for both personal and professional enrichment. Ministers may find that they learn about themselves and their ministry in most remarkable ways from those who are dying. A young priest was asked to say prayers with a woman in her eighties who was dying. He prayed with her and anointed her, and at that point was very startlingly aware that his training in college had taken him no further than this point. He felt very inadequate and scared and began to repeat the prayers which he had said already, as he admitted later to himself, to 'feel more comfortable' at the bedside of a dying person. It was his first encounter with death. His parishioner reached out and patted his hand. 'It's all right, you know,' she said. Her action changed the whole encounter, since they were caring for each other. Each felt able to offer something. Those involved in the hospice movement, which has developed the care of the dying so significantly, speak of how the dying patients in their care frequently helped and ministered to those who were officially caring for them.[8]

Two questions, we think, face the minister:

1 How can I manage just to be there when other people may be doing practical tasks?
2 How do I react personally, theologically and in my own spirituality to what is happening when someone with whom I am involved dies or when I am asked to take a funeral for someone whom I did not know?

More than most others, the minister represents a tradition which has tried over the centuries to provide some framework for integrating individuals into a larger framework of experience which attempts to make sense of fundamental issues. No two people have exactly the same story of their life to tell. Early experiences, parents, siblings, important relationships and losses colour the way in which we perceive or reject ideas of God. The Judeo-Christian tradition uses very personal language of fathers and sons, parents and children, brothers and sisters, and the minister brings the tradition with him by his presence.

Melvyn Thompson[9] explores three images of God commonly held, especially in the face of sickness and of death. The first is that God is indeed all-powerful and sends suffering as a way of punishing and keeping in order his Creation. God is understood as powerful but capricious. The second is that suffering is independent of God, who is loving and caring but impotent to do anything about it. The third is that God is involved with the forces of wholeness and integration in the face of illness and loss which has the power to disintegrate and destroy. The first two images are frequently those with which ministers may be endowed by those they come into contact with, and indeed (particularly in the second) may represent how they see themselves. They may be seen as representing an all-powerful but fundamentally uncaring God, or being well meaning but powerless, capable of only offering palliative words and gestures. It is much harder for the behaviour of the minister to model[10] the third view.[11] Certainly it demands much more, and involves more personal theological and spiritual risk-taking, because it involves having to look at areas which are not clear and logical and where feelings may seem to be pulling in opposite directions. One minute a terminally ill person may be speaking with a lot of emotion about their own death, and at the next planning next year's holiday. The clergy may receive from those whom they visit very mixed messages of acceptance and rejection. One of the authors passed by the bed of a very sick woman who said to him, 'I don't know why you have come,' but at the same time patted the bed in an invitation to him to sit down. When he had sat down she delivered a diatribe on the evils of organized religion but said at the end of the visit, 'You let me get angry with you, and stayed, and that helped.'

Sometimes the strong feelings aroused by grief can be expressed very forcibly to ministers and what they represent. On one occasion a minister who went to visit the parents of a child who had died in a road accident was met at the door by the mother rushing up and pummelling him. He did not leave the house but stayed and after a while the mother of the dead child put her arm on his shoulder and sobbed. What he seemed to do was to represent a God who did not exact retribution for her actions and strong feelings but who could stay with her physically and emotionally, not trying to change her or the situation but simply by being there.

Education for death

So far we have spoken of the work which clergy may do at the time of death and bereavement, and we shall return to this. But it may also be that the clergy will find their function with their parishioners or congregation involving raising the issues of death and bereavement in sermons and seminars and in informal groups. These groups should also ideally include contributions from general practitioners, funeral directors, solicitors and other caring agencies. The role of the laity as representatives in visiting the dying and bereaved, especially post-bereavement visits, should be raised. In a society which finds endings and death difficult subjects to face, these issues may be raised with the clergy, often very informally, by those other than the formally religious and in settings other than the sickroom or hospital. A hospital chaplain may well have a special task of developing with hospital staff (medical students, student nurses and others) some of the issues involved in caring for the dying and bereaved. This is an essential piece of work, although paradoxically the view of the clergy as the 'death experts' may be reinforced just at a time when the traditions among Christians about Unction and Communion of the Sick may be changing precisely so that the church and the clergy are not viewed as being concerned only with the moment of actual death.

Greater attention has been given to the role of bereavement care in clergy training, especially in pre-ordination training. This emphasis may help clergy to feel more confident to work collaboratively with others, such as funeral directors, lay volunteers and general practitioners.

Making contact

Obviously there will be a considerable diversity in the way ministers work with those whom they do not know well, and may only encounter at a time of crisis, compared with those who are in regular contact with them or the religious tradition they represent. With the former group of people the contacts they have may, in the early stages, consist of what might be called 'pre-counselling' and 'pre-evangelism'. It may take some time to find out exactly what are the feelings of the people concerned. How are they managing? What are their needs? For example, is their idea of resurrection the same as that of the minister? Language which may make considerable sense to the minister may not be experienced in the same way by others. Phrases like 'love of God' and 'being saved' may have a significance associated with public worship which may not be the same in another setting. At the same time, Truax and Carkhuff[12] list among the attributes of a good helper the qualities of *genuineness* and *congruence*, suggesting that to be clearly at ease between the externals of what one represents and the internals of what one believes is something which provides a helper's greatest asset. For the pastor who is ministering to the dying and bereaved this must involve facing personal questions: 'How do I feel about and face the possibility of my own death or of those close to me?' 'What are the points of contact inside myself between what I believe privately and express publicly?' 'Are the things I say, for example at funerals, the same things I learnt some time ago as an intellectual proposition?' 'How does my spirituality, what I believe and what I pray about, change or develop in the face of what I experience?'

More fundamentally, ministers may need to examine honestly their own need in the first place to enter a profession which is expected to cope with mortality and loss. What is sometimes called in psychological language *reaction forma-tion* suggests that one may be drawn in one's choice of job or occupation to face precisely those areas in one's own life and background which have been difficult, in order, as it were, to try and put those issues right at second hand through one's work. We are not talking about something which most of us 'know' consciously, but about something rather more hidden which will take some time and sensitivity to understand. Elizabeth Kubler-Ross tells of a student who denied any diffi-culty in facing dying people. When he was heavily pressed by his fellow students as to what he actually said it became clear that he did not go beyond the door of the room but just stood there and said 'God is love!'

There are three attributes which, properly used and under-stood, are an essential part of the way the minister comes close to those facing death, but which may become part of a system of *avoidance*:

1 A set-apartness, through ordination, can lead to the minister being seen as having more access to the truth than others, and as the trustee of special qualities which are set aside for those who display special goodness.
2 The different style of dress, and use of special language may, instead of being ways of making contact, become part of a *defensive* system which is basically self-protective, and which may make the minister less available.
3 The use of formal prayers and ritualized action may, instead of being a shared communication, protect the minister from a fuller relationship. Ritual is of its nature a general and pub-lic rather than specific and private way of communication.

The minister's 'business', real or imagined, can lead to the impression that the dying or bereaved are receiving a special bonus in his or her hurried visits.

A number of studies made of terminally ill patients suggest that a far larger group than might be imagined clearly realized their diagnosis.[13] They may not have admitted it to themselves or talked to a staff member if in hospital, still less to their family and friends, but subsequently they were able to pin-point very accurately when the diagnosis was made. The minister may well find that they are the one with whom the dying person, as one terminally ill man put it, 'tries on for size the possibility of his own death'. It is crucial for the minister to know what has been decided by those who are concerned with the care of the dying person. What decision has been made about informing that person of their prognosis? It will not usually be the minister who is concerned with 'telling the patient'. When, for example, relatives insist that the person must not be told what is happening, the minister may be able to say, 'Certainly your decision about telling him must be respected, but do you think that he might be trying to tell *you* something?'

Language which speaks clearly and comfortingly to some people will not be heard in the same way by others. 'One person's most precious phrases are another person's cant.' Sometimes theological statements with which Christians might concur if used in the context of worship, like 'God is love', are often alienating if used in a different context. The words may not then be seen as a statement about the nature of God and his Creation, but as attempting to justify the unjustifiable.[14] Religious activities and personnel are often seen as helping people to be 'good' and well adapted. Yet ministers who, by their presence and attitude, help people behave differently can sometimes let them react to loss in a way that does justice to how they may feel, but at the same time may develop and change their view of God.[15]

A single woman in mid-life developed a fast-growing tumour. During her final hospital admission she remarked to the minister who visited her how strange it was that she had written a poem to God which began 'You whom I have loved and given everything and now You have betrayed me,' and that she was also dreaming of children. She had been a long-standing communicant member of her church and had passed the age when having children was a possibility. Her minister, instead of replying to the unreasonableness of what she was saying and for which she was apologizing profusely since she felt it was 'wasting your time', listened for a while. He then said something about the place of anger and questioning as part of a Christian search for God and how often, especially when ill, one could look at unfulfilled possibilities in life and feel sad about them. She began to talk about what she called her 'half-open doors'. She went back over her life and thought aloud about the events which had never quite come about exactly as she had predicted them. She seemed to present at this point in her illness two ways of coping. To those who did not know her well she presented what was usually called 'a brave face'. To the minister she talked about her 'lost possibilities' until she could finally say that she had now faced them and could let them go into God's hands. The minister and she prayed together with 'letting go' as a theme. It was crucial for her to recover some vision of a God who understood her other imperfect feelings and who did not try to correct false impressions as she faced the end of her life. The minister did not at first find it at all easy to understand what she was saying. He had to struggle too.

Ministers are sometimes asked outright by the dying person or his relatives, 'Is this all there is? Shall we meet again?' To answer the question with integrity according to the people and circumstances involved needs considerable discernment. When and who asks that question and how it is asked may affect whether one gives an answer from Scripture or from one's own conviction or says something like, 'You must really miss him,' or, 'It's hard to let go people you love, isn't it?' The prospect of sharing in the resurrection of Jesus lies at the heart of the Christian gospel and it is that aspect of the Christian tradition from which countless dying and bereaved people derive their hope.

But other factors may make it difficult for that message to be heard. Pastoral experience and surveys[16] suggest that the continuation of life after death is viewed in a number of ways, not all informed by Christian tradition, in the population as a whole. A considerable interest in reincarnation, of growth and development through many rebirths, or mysticism 'undogmatic by nature and experimental in character'[17] is in stark contrast to the Christian hope of resurrection, as developed in the tradition of both the Old and New Testaments.[18] One study[19] raises cogently the problem of preaching and speaking of the resurrection against such a confused background of belief and non-belief. The author tells the story of a family who wished the ashes of their father to be scattered on the local football pitch so that he could catch continuously the atmosphere of each Saturday's match. This story illustrates poignantly, and reflects with some accuracy, a popular view of what happens at death. In spite of everything, things turn out all right and we survive, in some form, either to enjoy what death snatched away from us in this life or to experience a reversal of life's injustices, like Lazarus in the parable which Jesus told (Luke 16.19–31). Basic to this popular belief about life after death is the separation of soul and body and the immortality of the soul. Almost every *In Memoriam* column in the local paper provides evidence of this. 'Gentle Jesus up above, give our granny all our love.' Parents tell their children that granny has become an angel, even if that is hardly how they would have described her when she was alive. Our loved ones leave behind their bodies and go to a life where all is well, the inheritance of all sincere people who have kept the golden rule.

There is, of course, an important theological and pastoral distinction to be made. *Revivification* implies the person will come back to life just as they were. *Resurrection* is essentially a doctrine which encompasses the future and does not involve using the past as a basis for understanding the present or the future.

> A great deal of our difficulty when considering the future life is that we apply to it the logic of desire, instead of the logic of hope. We take it for granted that the form of our fulfilment in the future life will be modelled on what we desire as the people we are now. And this generally makes what we call heaven either ridiculous or frankly incredible or patently the projection of our own wishes onto the sky. But hope is the prospect of the radically new. It is the breaking in of what we had never dreamed of, a fulfilment beyond our desire to conceive.[20]

Peter Selby's[21] exploration of the resurrection themes stresses the importance of the resurrection of Jesus as perceived corporately, to make sense of the future. The dialogue between Geoffrey Lampe and Donald McKinnon[22] sensitively discusses the resurrection of Jesus, while pointing out the danger of Christians appearing to offer a trivialized doctrine of what Lampe calls 'a corpse raised to life'. The pastoral implications of this debate are considerable.

The current confusion of attitudes which we have indicated makes the discussion even more germane and of considerable importance to the minister who cares for the dying and bereaved. A woman whose husband had suddenly died said to a minister colleague six weeks or so after his death, 'Something wonderful happened today. I forgot John.' She did not mean that she had ceased at that point to love him or miss him, but she had been terrified even to sleep lest her husband should disappear from her conscious memory. She found that she could forget him for moments when, for example, she was involved with her children, but she could also know that he was not completely lost to her. As she put it, 'his image can stay inside me', and her relief was immense. Her continuing love for her husband, and her sense of being close to him did not depend on her conscious effort.

The need to explore what is behind our understanding of the resurrection is an essential part of the minister's responsibility. But a balance needs to be maintained, and it is sometimes easy to give the impression that the physical body, or tangible needs, are of no interest to the minister.

> Because the clergy are often viewed as on the side of the spirit with either a disregard of, or a turning away from, the physical side of life, it is important to articulate the goodness of the body and its important role in the whole economy of God. There is a need to be reminded that the creation story describes the creation of the world as 'good', and the creation of man from the dust of the earth as 'very good'. Man does not have a body or a soul. Rather, man is a body or he is a soul depending on the perspective at the moment from which he is viewed. Jesus's words, 'I thirst,' are a reminder of the physical side of life to both patient and pastor.[23]

Does churchmanship matter?

There is no easy answer to this question. Most ministers obviously need to work inside a tradition, since that usually provides them with their fixed points, some of their language and a system of familiar and significant words and actions. Their pastoral skill will come in their perception of how much the resources they bring are of real or potential value to those with whom they may come into contact, or whether those resources may be a hindrance to meeting people at a more than superficial level. How does one stand with integrity by some positions, but manage to be flexible about others? Are there other actions or words which can make the same point without distorting the meaning of what the minister may understand as vital? A seriously ill man from an evangelical Christian background in which free prayer was the norm was very appreciative of the ministry of the local vicar who came from a very different background because, as he said, 'he uses prayers from a book but they could be meant for me.'

In Chapter 5 we discussed the place of rites of passage, and the clergy are usually at the centre of, or much involved with, the rituals of dying and mourning. Being able to 'get it right' and to offer a liturgical form in terms of service at a crematorium or later at a memorial service may be more important than any other actions or words. A theological college principal once said to his students, correctly we believe, 'Taking funerals may be one of the most important pastoral functions you will ever perform.'

The personal relations of the minister

Ministers may frequently develop very fulfilling relationships with people who are facing death, and may feel at times that they are really doing the job for which they were ordained. But at other times the relationship may be more difficult to understand, especially if a person is expressing towards the minister or others strong emotions which are sometimes conflicting, of hate or love, or by apparently being very dependent and unable to make a decision without reference to the minister. It is not within the scope of this book to deal with some of the strong feelings which may take place in a pastoral relationship, except to remember that the representative role of ministers and their special access to people in crisis may lead to them being seen (or seeing themselves) as endowed with particular qualities.

The psychological term 'transference' is a useful one, since it means that ministers may be seen not just as themselves.[24] In a situation of loss, a minister's presence and sometimes their words can bring to the surface strong feelings which may belong, at an earlier stage of human growth and development, to another person, for example, father, mother or teacher. The minister in turn may be surprised by the strength of personal feeling about the people for whom he or she is caring. They too may acquire significance and come to represent people who have been an important part of the minister's own past and background. We should stress that these feelings do not mean that the minister is doing a bad job, or that it is a situation from which one ought to withdraw rapidly. Properly understood it can provide a very useful and important way of caring more effectively.[25]

A very simple model of helping is that offered by Gerard Egan and shown in Figure 3. It encourages the helper to reflect, either individually or with the one seeking help, in order to clarify what is happening in the relationship or in relation to the problem being presented. To facilitate this reflection Egan suggests a cycle or process through which one 'explores' the issue presented in order to come to some mutual 'understanding' on the basis of which one formulates possible 'options'. These options can then be 'explored' in turn in order to understand their helpfulness or otherwise. This may then lead to other options being identified and explored, etc. In order to help this process one would use the basic counselling skills of attending, listening and responding. This helping process can be used with the other person or within oneself to enable better understanding within the carer of what might be happening.

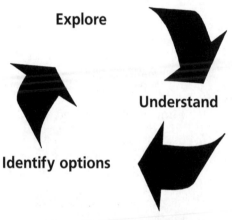

Explore

Understand

Identify options

Figure 3. A model of helping

The minister's crucial role in bereavement or terminal illness may lead either to over-involvement, where it becomes difficult to distinguish between one's own needs and those of others, or to withdrawal, perhaps feeling that everybody is becoming too dependent upon the minister. Overprotectiveness is another danger and a good rule of caring is not to take away from anybody, however ill or distraught, the ability to do things which, with support, they might hope to do for themselves. Alternatively ministers might feel that they only have something to offer to a dying or bereaved person if they bring something tangible when they visit. One widowed man, when asked if his vicar had visited him, replied with irritation, 'Yes, he came two or three times a week at first, but always with a little present. It was as if he found it hard to come by himself.'

Who supports the minister?

It is often easy to behave as if the giving of help is somehow a more worthwhile activity than the receiving of help, so the needs of ministers caring for the dying may be neglected by themselves and by others. How ministers recognize their own feelings and needs will deeply affect the way in which they cope. The burial service makes it clear that one of its functions is to remind those present, minister included, of their own mortality.

The question, 'What does the grief of others do to you?' is one to which we believe each minister has to be helped to find their own answer. As we have indicated, no two ministers will cope identically. Some may share their vulnerability with their families; others with their colleagues; others may bottle them up, perhaps only emerging to speak of crematorium fees as 'ash cash'! To manage well the pastoral care of the terminally ill and the bereaved is to face the question as to how much each person is prepared to allow painful and difficult experiences to reach them. When asked whether the constant experience of death ever 'got to' him, an experienced hospital chaplain remarked that if it did not move him just a little each time then he had no business doing his job.

Putting succinctly the idea of controlled involvement, T. S. Eliot wrote, 'Teach us to care and not to care'.[27] There are again lessons to be learnt here from the hospice movement[28] where the support of staff in groups and individually is seen as of prime importance. This does not always work as effectively as would be hoped and 'chronic niceness', with an emphasis on perfect caring, can ensue.[29] Clergy can also be very prone to this and appraisal systems should include reflection on expectations (internal and external) and how realistic they are. Within the NHS and other caring groups the development of the National Association for Staff Support[30] has been an important acknowledgement that carers do not always receive the nurturing they require if they are to continue offering good care to others.

Some dioceses[31] have developed a network of support groups for clergy and pastoral workers which meet regularly and are one very valuable resource where those involved in pastoral care have been able to talk in confidence with a group of peers and raise some of their own needs for support. Individual needs are obviously very different, but we would stress that those clergy who obtain support and supervision are frequently those who manage best in situations like death which involve so closely the relationship between the personality, spirituality and practice of the minister.

Peer review can often be a helpful way of receiving feedback and of monitoring performance. In some instances, for example, a colleague may sit in on a funeral and then provide feedback later. On another occasion the roles may be reversed so that the observer is then observed. Developing confidence in one's own role is helpful when working with members of other professions because one is less likely to feel threatened by perceived competence in the other, although this feeling might not actually match what they are feeling themselves.

Clergy are frequently able to make links between other people who may be involved in the care of the dying and the bereaved, bringing together others, doctors, nurses and social workers, possibly by means of a monthly bread and cheese lunch, frequently on church premises, arranged by the local clergy.

While we have concentrated in this chapter on ministers and their ways of working and particular needs, we would not want to suggest that the pastoral care is an exclusive function of ordained ministers. Much care to the dying and the bereaved is also given by lay people, and it would be presumptuous to imagine that ministers have a monopoly of pastoral skill or resources.

There may be occasions when a minister has become very attached to a particular parishioner who is dying and to the family. When that person dies the minister will also share in the sense of loss and experience the pain of letting go. Because of their profession ministers may feel that they should be 'above' such feelings and, therefore, deny their own grief. If there are a series of such losses there can be an accumulation of unresolved grief with consequent need for personal support.

Appropriate appraisal has been slow in entering ministerial practice. There is no single universally agreed definition of appraisal. It may be better to think of it more as a philosophy than a clearly defined process. But appraisal, as carried out in individual performance review (IPR), will be familiar to chaplains and others who work in organizations such as the NHS or in education and is increasingly a part of ministerial review. Appraisal tries to create a shared vision between the individual and the organization they serve, helping that person understand and recognize their own part in bringing that vision about, and bringing about training and supervision to undergird the whole process. Performance review is never a package solution but needs to be developed carefully with the individual concerned. It has links to how the person wishes to take their training forward and what personal development they may need. A number of Church of England dioceses and other Churches have developed forms of ministerial appraisal which are not formally 'hierarchical', and we believe these are of particular value in helping clergy and ministers develop their ministry, especially with the bereaved and dying.[32]

It can be tempting to take clergy and other caring people for granted and to assume that they do not have needs. Because of this they may suppress such needs and see them as inappropriate to their role. One valuable source of support for the clergyman should be the local Christian community and other members of the caring professions. However, we should not overlook the very valuable contribution that the patient can make in helping *us* to face the reality of death. If we couple this support with the words of St Paul, 'Not that we are sufficient of ourselves to claim anything as coming from us; our sufficiency is from God,'[33] we may learn to integrate death into our experience of living and thus find the 'courage to be'[34] with the dying and the bereaved.

Notes

1 See S. Payne and M. Relph, 'The assessment of need for bereavement follow-up in palliative and hospice care', *Palliative Medicine*. 8 (1994) pp. 291–97.

2 J. Hinton, *Dying* (Penguin, 2nd edn 1972).

3 See, for example, 'Spirituality' in *The New Dictionary of Medical Ethics*, eds. Boyd, Higgs and Pinching (BMJ, 1997); and P. Speck, chapter on 'Spiritual Care' in *Oxford Textbook of Palliative Medicine*, eds. Doyle, Hanks and MacDonald (Oxford University Press, 1998).

4 Church of England *Alternative Service Book*, p. 356.

5 Genesis 3.9.

6 The Bishop of Southwark's Advisory Committee for Pastoral Care and Counselling, Occasional Newsletter 1979.

7 R. J. Kastenbaum and R. Aisenberg, *The Psychology of Death* (Duckworth, 1974).

8 S. Stoddard, *The Hospice Movement* (Cape, 1979).

9 M. Thompson, *Cancer and the God of Love* (SCM, 1976).

10 By modelling we mean simply behaviour which may make what a person stands for more easily visible to others.

11 See John Hick, *Evil and the God of Love* (Macmillan, 1966) for an exposition of this third view.

12 C. B. Truax and R. R. Carkhuff, *Toward Effective Counselling and Psychotherapy* (Aldine Publishers, 1967).

13 Ian Ainsworth-Smith, 'At the Front Line of Dying', *Journal of Community Nursing* (October 1977).

14 C. S. Lewis, *A Grief Observed*: 'Talk to me about the comforts of religion and I shall suspect you don't understand.'

15 This becomes an opportunity for growth, as described in Chapter 1.

16 For example, the Opinion Research Centre study commissioned by the BBC into belief in life after death. *Sunday Telegraph* (13 October 1974).

17 I. Bunting, *Preaching at Funerals* (Grove Booklet No. 62, Bramcote, Notts., 1978), pp. 7–9.

18 1 Corinthians 15.44: 'It is sown a physical body, it is raised a spiritual body.'

19 Bunting, op. cit.

20 H. A. Williams, *True Resurrection* (Mitchell Beazley, 1972).

21 P. Selby, *Look for the Living* (SCM, 1975).

22 G. W. H. Lampe and D. H. McKinnon, *The Resurrection* (Mowbray, 1966).

23 B. Schoenberg *et al.*, *Psychosocial Aspects of Terminal Care* (Columbia University Press, 1972).

24 For further discussion of how the minister may cope with situations calling for specific counselling skills see H. Clinebell, *Basic Types of Pastoral Counselling* (Abingdon, 1966); E. Kennedy, *On Becoming a Counsellor* (Gill and Macmillan, 1977); M. Jacobs, *Still Small Voice* (SPCK, 1982).

25 A teenager's 'crush' on the curate would be a good example of this.

26 G. Egan, *The Skilled Helper: Models, Skills and Methods for Effective Helping.* 2nd edn (Brooks/Cole, 1982).

27 T. S. Eliot, 'Ash Wednesday – I', *Collected Poems 1909–1962* (Faber 1963).

28 S. Stoddard, op. cit.; see also an article with the rather sensational title 'Counteracting Burn-out for the Hospice Care-giver' by M. Friel and C. Tehan in *Cancer Nursing* (August 1980) which provides some excellent suggestions for supporting professional and voluntary helpers.

29 P. Speck, 'Unconscious processes'. *Palliative Medicine.* 10 (1996) pp. 273–74.

30 The National Association for Staff Support (NASS) can be contacted at 9 Carodon Close, Woking, Surrey GU21 3DU (Tel: 01483 771599).

31 Notably developed in the Dioceses of Southwark, London, Rochester, Chichester and St Albans.

32 *Ministerial Review: its purpose and practice. The report of a working*

party on clergy appraisal. ABM Ministry Paper No. 6 (Central Board of Finance of the Church of England, January 1994).

33 2 Corinthians 3.5.

34 P. Tillich, *The Courage to Be* (Fontana, 1979). Alastair Campbell, *Rediscovering Pastoral Care* (Darton, Longman and Todd, 1981), pp. 26-64, gives a sensitive development of three biblical images, the shepherd's courage, the healer's wounds and the fool's wisdom. He suggests that the minister's ability to represent these images and to explore the meaning behind them is crucial both to their integrity and to their ability to help others.

APPENDIX A

Practicalities

The formalities and practicalities connected with death can seem daunting, so we would like to examine a few 'nuts and bolts' issues, not with a view to answering all the questions, but indicating where might be the best source of further help.

The hospice movement

The modern hospice has become a skilled community which aims at improving the quality of life remaining for patients with long-term as well as mortal illnesses and sometimes for the frail and elderly. It accepts the patient with his family as the focus of its concern, involving them where possible as part of the caring team and supporting them in their bereavement.[1]

The word 'hospice' has a long history reminiscent at times of its medieval origins in feeding and housing those who were on a journey. 'Deep in our common mind and heart, as old as our civilization itself is the knowledge that hospitality is a duty owed to the weary traveller and to the sick.'[2]

The effect of hospices on care, not just of dying people, has been considerable, and has challenged widely held notions of success and failure in caring for the sick. Michael Wilson[3] and others have written how the curing of disease is frequently viewed as a more valuable activity than caring for those whose physical condition may not be curable but whose need for care is considerable. The *raison d'être* of the hospice movement is a better understanding of the nature of terminal pain and its relief. It is also attentive to the need for sensitive, imaginative and skilled personal care so that the dying person can live to the utmost of their ability and potential, physically, psychologically and spiritually. Hospices in the United Kingdom have developed partly from the pioneer work of institutions like St Joseph's Hospice, Hackney, and the Hostel of God, Clapham (now called Trinity Hospice), and especially from the work and experience of Dame Cicely Saunders and St Christopher's Hospice, Sydenham.

In recent years there have been great changes in this area of care, with the development of specialist palliative care and a complete review in the UK of the provision of cancer services, access to specialist palliative care and the extension of the palliative care approach to non-cancerous conditions. Palliative care teams now exist in many acute hospitals or communities and patients who suffer from a variety of symptoms as a result of their disease or treatment may benefit from a palliative care approach. Patients with life-threatening illness can have more choice over where they die, and a greater control over how they approach their own death and over the life that is left.

This may all happen without the person setting foot inside a specialist palliative care facility such as a hospice. The emphasis on a collaborative (multi-professional) approach, wherever the patient is being cared for, means that pastoral care has a key role, provided that those offering their services can be reasonably clear about what they have to offer. This involves taking a wider remit than purely the provision of a religious ministry in order to journey with the dying person in an appropriate way for them.

One disturbing aspect of the development of palliative care, however, is that as health care moves towards 'evidence-based' medicine it tends to be easier to obtain funding for symptom-relief programmes and clinical interventionist approaches than for psycho-social, spiritual or other holistic aspects of care. This could lead to a split between palliative medicine (as symptomatology) and palliative care (perceived as the 'soft' side of care). It is important to maintain the inter-relatedness of care, and clergy will need to be able to demonstrate the effectiveness of pastoral care as a key component of holistic care lest it become squeezed out in favour of funding more measurable aspects.[4]

Many of the people who turn to specialist palliative care are looking for the relief of a variety of distressing symptoms, but they are also looking for personalized care which contains a greater recognition of values and beliefs than they may find in the busier acute setting.

Making a will

Details on the making of a will and managing the estate of a person who has died are clearly set out in a Consumers' Association booklet.[5] The National Council for Voluntary Organizations also produces a pamphlet dealing with death which offers practical and concise advice, not only about making a will but also other practical details.[6] They also indicate the point at which the help of a solicitor may be needed.[7] Information and advice on making a will or settling an estate can be obtained from a local Citizens' Advice Bureau. A local Social Security office will give information on the help available in the form of death grant and other benefits.

What to do when someone dies

There are a number of procedures and formalities like registering the death and contacting a funeral director which should take place as soon as possible. An excellent guide to the practicalities is provided in the Consumers' Association booklet, *What to do when someone dies*.[8] Figure 4 is taken from that publication and demonstrates the stages of registering a death and arranging a funeral. One point to bear in mind is that if a cremation is envisaged, an extra medical certificate will be required from a medical practitioner who is not in partnership with the patient's own doctor. If death takes place at home this is something which the funeral director can arrange, and if in hospital a further certificate can be arranged on request.

Post-mortem examination

The doctor who attended a person before death, either at home or in hospital, will usually issue a medical certificate showing the cause of death and a formal notice of death can be taken to the Registrar of Births and Deaths for registration. A post-mortem examination may be requested by the doctor if the nearest relatives agree. A typical form of consent which gives the usual reasons for the request is as follows:

I do not object to a post-mortem examination being carried out on the body of . . . and I am not aware that he/she had expressed objection or that another relative objects.

I understand that this examination is carried out:

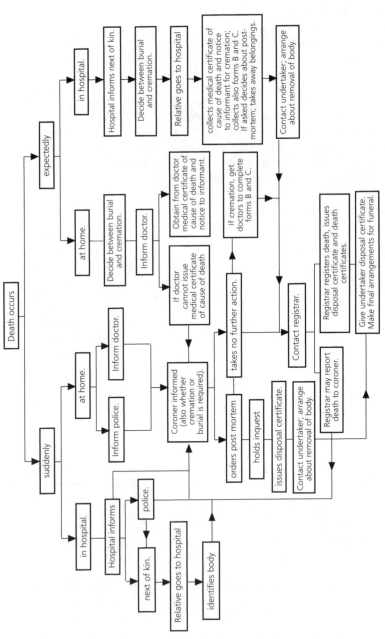

Figure 4. What to do when someone dies

(a) to verify the cause of death and to study the effects of treatment, which may involve the retention of tissue for laboratory study.

(b) to remove amounts of tissue for the treatment of other patients and for medical education and research.

The post-mortem examination usually takes place very shortly after death so it is rare for funeral arrangements to be affected.

The coroner

The attending doctor may report the death to the coroner (a doctor or lawyer responsible for investigating certain deaths).[9] The coroner is usually informed if (a) the dead person was not attended by a doctor during his last illness or within 14 days of death; (b) the cause of death is uncertain; (c) the cause of death was sudden, violent or due to an accident; (d) death was caused by a notifiable industrial disease; (e) death took place during or immediately after a surgical procedure. The coroner will usually arrange for a post-mortem examination of the body. The relatives' consent is not required but they may nominate a doctor of their choice to be present. If the death was shown to be due to natural causes he will issue a notification of death to be handed to the Registrar of Births and Deaths. If the death was violent or accidental, caused by an industrial disease or if, after post-mortem examination, the cause of death remains uncertain, the coroner will hold an inquest. This is quite simply an inquiry into the cause and circumstances of the death. The inquest is held in public and the coroner may direct that a jury hear the case. The relatives of the dead person may wish to be legally represented at the coroner's inquest and this is particularly advisable if death follows an accident or industrial disease.

It is rare for an inquest to delay funeral arrangements by more than a few days, if at all. But it should be borne in mind that a funeral cannot take place without the coroner's authorization. However, once the inquest has been opened and evidence of identification taken the coroner may well adjourn the inquest to a later date to allow further investigation to be made. Under those circumstances he will usually issue a form of authorization for a funeral to take place. He can also issue, on request, a letter confirming the fact of death for legal or social security purposes.

Donation of a body for medical research

A person may wish to bequeath their body after death for anatomical research. It is advisable for someone contemplating this course of action to check that their near relatives have no objection. Application (for England and Wales) should be made to: H. M. Inspector of Anatomy, Alexander Fleming House, London SE1 6BY – from whom a form of consent can be obtained which should be signed and witnessed and placed with other personal papers where it can be found after death. Alternatively the Professor of Anatomy at the local teaching hospital/medical school will be able to advise those considering donation.

Anatomical examination may extend over a period of up to two years. Once it is complete arrangements are usually made by the medical school concerned for a service of burial or cremation of the body conducted by a minister of the faith held by the deceased person in life. The next of kin can be informed of the date and time of the funeral if they wish.

As soon as possible after death the Inspector of Anatomy should be informed by the deceased person's executors or next of kin.

No guarantee can be given by the Inspector of Anatomy that a donation can be accepted. The place of death and the cause of death are two factors which may affect the decision. A body from which organs have been removed for transplantation is not usually accepted for anatomical research.

I (full name, block capitals)

request that after my death
* (a) any parts of my body be used for medical
    purposes; or
* (b) my *kidneys, *eyes, *heart, *liver, *pituitary
    gland, *pancreas be used for medical
    purposes.
* (delete if not applicable)

Signature   Date

In the event of my death, if possible contact:

Name (block capitals)   Telephone number

Figure 5. Example of a donor card

Donation of organs for transplantation

The former Department of Health and Social Security issued in December 1979[10] a Code of Practice which hoped to increase the supply of kidneys and other organs for transplantation. The relevant legislation[11] remains basically a system of 'opting in', usually by means of a card (see example in Figure 5) carried by the person which gives consent to the removal of specified tissue or organs (for example, kidneys, heart and eye corneas) after death. Particular attention needs to be paid to relatives feeling that they have a free and non-pressurized choice when there is any question of organ donation. It should be remembered that as the law in the UK stands at the moment it is at least theoretically possible that relatives could make a valid refusal to donate organs, even if the person concerned had been carrying a donor card. Practice is changing rapidly and there is ongoing discussion nationally regarding the most effective method for obtaining organs for transplantation, as well as the timing of such requests.

The Code of Practice clarifies the clinical definition of 'brain stem death' and discusses how a patient's relatives should best be approached for permission to remove organs for transplantation. Transplantation is most likely to be successful if organs are removed from a body as soon as possible after death has been certified.[12]

Every transplant team in the UK contains a coordinator whose training initially is as a nurse, usually with extensive experience of working in an intensive care unit. Among their other duties the coordinator may provide a link between the 'donor' family and the recipient of a transplanted organ. The coordinator may on occasions provide information for the donor family, should they request it, on how the organs have been used. Naturally the sharing of this information would not reveal names, or other identifying details of the recipients. Hospital chaplains often liaise closely with the coordinators when offering pastoral care to families in intensive care.

Notes

1 C. Saunders, 'Hospices', in *Dictionary of Medical Ethics* (Darton, Longman and Todd, 1981).
2 R. Lamerton, *Care of the Dying* (Penguin, 1980), p.16.
3 M. Wilson, *Health is for People* (Darton, Longman and Todd, 1976).
4 See M. King, P. Speck and A. Thomas, 'Spiritual and religious

beliefs in acute illness – is this a feasible area for study?' *Social Science and Medicine* 38 (1994), pp. 631–6; and P. Speck, 'Working with dying people: on being good enough', in A. Obholzer and V. Roberts, *The Unconscious at Work: Individual and Organizational Stress in the Human Services* (Routledge, 1994).

5 *Wills and Probate*, Consumers' Association.

6 W. M. Bowder, *Dealing with Death* (National Council for Voluntary Organisations, 26 Bedford Square, London WC1, 1980).

7 The names of solicitors who practise in a neighbourhood can be obtained from The Law Society (113 Chancery Lane, London WC2A 1PL) or from a Citizens' Advice Bureau.

8 *What to Do When Someone Dies* (Consumers' Association 1998).

9 In Scotland and Northern Ireland the procedures are different.

10 *The Removal of Cadaveric Organs for Transplantation – A Code of Practice* (HMSO, 1979).

11 Human Tissue Act 1961, 9 and 10 Eliz. 2, ch. 54.

12 R. Calne, 'Tissue Transplantation' in *Dictionary of Medical Ethics* (Darton, Longman and Todd, 1981).

APPENDIX B

Useful Addresses

Sue Ryder Foundation, Cavendish, Sudbury, Suffolk CO10 8AY (Tel. 01787 280252).
Cares for the physically and mentally ill, elderly and mentally handicapped people in residential homes.

Cruse Bereavement Care,126 Sheen Road, Richmond, Surrey TW9 1UR (Tel. 0181 940 4818; Helpline 0181 332 7227).
The national association for the widowed and their children.

Child Bereavement Trust, Harleyford Estate, Henley Road, Marlow SL7 2DX (Tel. 01628 488101).
Training and resources for professionals.

The Compassionate Friends, The Administration Office, 53 North Street, Bristol BS3 1EN (Tel. 0117 966 5202; Helpline 0117 953 9639).
A society of parents who have themselves experienced the loss of a child which seeks to help and support those whose children have died.

Stillbirth and Neonatal Death Society (SANDS), 28 Portland Place, London W1N 4DE (Tel. 0171 436 5881).
Supports those families whose children have been stillborn or died in infancy, and seeks to increase the awareness of those who come into contact with parents and relatives after the death of a baby.

Foundation for the Study of Infant Deaths (FSID), 14 Halkin Street, London SW1X 7DP (Tel. 0171 235 0965; Helpline 0171 235 1721).
Seeks to develop research into neonatal mortality.

Age Concern England, Astral House, 1268 London Road, London SW16 4ER (Tel. 0181 679 8000).
A major voluntary organization concerned with the needs of the elderly, including bereavement.

Support around Termination for Abnormality (SATFA), 73 Charlotte Street, London W1P 1LB (Tel. 0171 631 0280; Helpline 0171 631 0285).
Helping parents who discover that their unborn child is abnormal.

National Association of Bereavement Services, 20 Norton Folgate, London E1 6DB (Tel. 0171 247 0617; Helpline 0171 247 1080).
Locally organized projects which offer practical and emotional support to the bereaved, and also train and supervise volunteers.

Facilities for cancer patients

An excellent annual directory of hospice and palliative care services is provided by the Hospice Information Service at St Christopher's Hospice, 51–59 Lawrie Park Road, London SE26 6DZ (Tel. 0181 778 9252). A small annual charge is made for registration to this valuable service.

Rehabilitation services for cancer patients

Colostomy
Colostomy Welfare Group
38–39 Eccleston Square (2nd Floor), London SW1V 1PB
(Tel. 0171 828 5175)

Laryngectomy
The National Association of Laryngectomy Clubs
Fourth Floor, Michael Sobell House, 30 Dorset Square, London NW1 6QL (Tel. 0171 402 6007)

Mastectomy
Mastectomy Association
25 Brighton Road, South Croydon, Surrey CR2 6EA (Tel. 0181 654 8643)

APPENDIX C

Some Other Cultural Patterns

The rituals associated with death, more than many other rites of passage, are closely identified with religion. The views held by the group concerning an after-life and the future mode of existence for the deceased will affect the ways in which the dead are disposed of.

From the beginning of time man has been the only creature known to bury his dead as an expression of his understanding of the nature and destiny of man. Archaeological findings indicate that when Neanderthal man died he was decently interred with ornament shells and stone implements, which he presumably might require beyond the grave. The positioning of some corpses in a fetal position may reflect a belief in rebirth. The binding of corpses, however, may well indicate a fear of the dead and of their powers to harm, especially if the burial rites had not been properly performed. Linked to this we have the stigma which attaches to leaving the dead unburied.

The stigma of leaving unburied dead relatives and friends, so much explored in classical literature and elsewhere, can be difficult to understand today when, if no one else can be found who was close to the dead person, funerals are arranged and paid for by local authorities or hospitals. Sophocles's play *Antigone* takes up vividly the theme of a sister who takes terrible risks to bury her dead brothers. The Aeneid tells of the unburied dead who cluster around Aeneas on his journey to the underworld, unable to cross the Styx and find rest. Similarly after a regiment of British infantry was virtually annihilated in the Zulu War of 1879 at Isandhlwana, the two surviving companies who were quartered some distance away insisted that the job of burying the dead was theirs. Closeknit groups like regiments, medieval guilds and the early Friendly Societies saw their duties to dead members incorporating both the care of widows and children and the provision of an appropriate funeral.

The two themes which arise in the stories seem to relate to fundamental needs in the mourners, which the funeral rituals try to meet. First there is the need for *reparation*, to have some ritual way of putting things right with and for the dead person, for ritual is a crucial way of 'acting the unsayable', especially where the circumstances of the death have been felt, because of accident, defeat or disaster, to be too terrible for words. Second there is the need for *propitiation*, to put things right so that the dead person and/or the gods cannot rebuke or even punish the living who have not done their proper duty by the dead.

We should emphasize that we do not believe that these themes represent beliefs that are consciously held by most people in the late twentieth century, but we are certain that the feelings ministers may encounter frequently among newly bereaved people may only be understandable if they themselves understand the fundamental and timeless issues which the old myths try to explore.

Perhaps the most obvious example of elaborate burial rituals is that found in ancient Egypt. Before 3100 BC, in the Pre-Dynastic period, graves were shallow pits in the sand into which the contracted body was placed together with a few grave goods. The use of coffins later led to decomposition of the body, which in turn led the Egyptians to develop the art of mummification. Because the Egyptians believed that the physical body would be needed in the next life it was important to preserve it. The coffins frequently had painted scenes inside and out. These paintings and inscriptions usually included objects of use to the deceased in the next life, plus magical texts to safeguard the deceased on their journey through the underworld as well as to ensure their continued existence. The provisions for the next life sometimes extended to ensuring that certain deceased people might avoid *posthumous* conscription to assist with land reclamation on the Nile. Thus Deputies were provided in burials from the Middle Kingdom onwards in the form of *shabtis*. These people were mummified and given hoes, mattocks and baskets. It was believed that they could magically come back to life, because of the spell written on them, and dig the fields and irrigate the land in the name of their dead owners.[1]

The belief that the dead are going on a journey and therefore need provisions and a safe passage are reflected in other cultures. Burial excavations have shown that the Vikings buried their dead with objects used in life and that the ship was commonly associated with their burials to indicate the journey. For a discussion of the anthropology and sociology associated with the variations to be found in the mode of disposal of dead bodies the studies of Douglas Davies[2] and Dewi Rees[3] are very helpful. The various cultural influences are examined, together with discussion of the way in which our death rites have changed and the implications for present and future practice. Rees includes a useful chapter on near death experiences, in which he describes the phenomenon and provides some thoughts about causation from his standpoint as a doctor of medicine. From a Christian viewpoint, a book edited by Jupp and Rogers[4] looks at the issues associated with Christian funerals from both a theological and liturgical perspective.

If the earthly body is of no further use after death then there is no need to go to elaborate lengths to preserve it. Hence those religions and cultures which believe in reincarnation, or in the continuing existence of the spirit freed from the limitations of the body, are free to dispose of the body by fire. Buddhism, Hinduism and Sikhism all practise cremation and this is carried out with due respect for what the body has conveyed and expressed in life. Muslims and Jews for the most part practise burial although some liberal and reformed Jews may agree to cremation. In Christianity both burial and cremation are practised.

The rituals associated with death and dying do not replace the grief process but rather are offered as a helpful structure. The dying person, the deceased, the survivor and his social environment may find in the ritual an expressive act which will *aid the normal process of grief* and the status transition of both the bereaved and the deceased.[5]

An interesting example of this use of ritual is that seen in the patterns of mourning among the Yolngu of Australia, which illustrates the effects of urbanization on established cultural patterns.

The Yolngu[6] are Australian Aborigines who live in north-eastern Arnhem Land, Northern Territory. In this area many clans have moved out of the town and have 'gone home', and this has led to a cultural revival. However, the ancient rituals have had to be modified because of modern hygiene laws and urban influences.

The ritual commences before the death with people gathering to sing clan songs to comfort the dying and to keep his mind alert so that he may die in the right way. Frequently there is keening (or wailing).

When death occurs there is a dramatic change in emotional tenor of the group. The widow and other close kin throw themselves on the body, screaming and crying uncontrollably in their grief. Others are quiet. The senior men announce the death, which is not openly acknowledged until the announcement. The women keen loudly, throw themselves on the ground and cut themselves on stones. The men may cry but usually express anger, which may lead to revenge attacks on other groups who are suspected of sorcery. The burial ceremony does not take place until everyone has arrived (a long time in Australia with large distances).

When the ceremonies have been arranged the body is collected from the hospital mortuary and taken, ceremonially, to the village. Car horns are sounded, there is singing and dancing. The body is placed in a shelter (usually in a large commercial refrigerator) which becomes the focal point for the community songs and dances. These songs act to effect *separation* for the deceased so that the spirit can travel to its right resting place. The lid of the coffin is decorated with sacred clan designs by the senior men, who alone see them.

Traditionally the body was placed on a platform for the birds to pick the bones clean prior to burial. Nowadays that is not allowed. The burial is accompanied by singing and dancing and a short ceremony conducted by a Christian minister. After he has gone some of the men return to 'switch' with leaves of burning branches to chase away the spirit. Those concerned with the burial are unclean and require ritual washing. Several months or even years later further ceremonies may be held to cleanse the house of the deceased for habitation. Traditionally the bones would be recovered, cleaned, placed in a bark coffin, which was decorated and placed upright (as a totem) exposed to the elements until eventually it decayed away. This is no longer widely practised in Arnhem Land, but sufficient of the ritual is retained in modified form to facilitate the grieving of the relative.

Mourning for the Yolngu is structured, guided and limited and it is expected to be publicly expressed. The reality of the death is clearly demonstrated to the bereaved and expression of emotional reaction encouraged, with visible social support. In the conclusion of her article on the Yolngu, Janice Reid writes:

'In northeastern Arnhem Land the mortuary ceremonies not only affirm in dramatic form the relations and beliefs of the living, but enable the bereaved to mourn in a culturally structured and contained context, to resolve grief and to resume social roles. In short, mortuary ceremonies afford the bereaved "a time to live" and "a time to grieve".'

While the traditions of the Yolngu may not be applicable to our own culture, the way in which they employ ritual and have adapted not dispensed with it in the face of urbanization, has much to say to us in our management of grief.

The work of anthropologists is not confined to rummaging among old bones, but can illuminate our understanding of why we feel a need to perform certain actions in our progressive twentieth century, the reasons for which have often been lost in the mist of time.[7] Connecting with these earlier reasons can be very important and fulfilling, as evidenced in the rediscovery of the Celtic influences in Christianity.

Notes

1 British Museum Guide (1976), p. 35ff.
2 D. Davies, *Death, Ritual and Belief: The Rhetoric of Funerary Rites* (Cassell, 1997).
3 D. Rees, *Death and Bereavement: The Psychological, Religious and Cultural Interfaces* (Whurr, 1997).
4 P. Jupp and T. Rogers, *Interpreting Death: Christian Theology and Pastoral Practice* (Cassell, 1997).
5 For an excellent historical perspective of customs, literature and rituals from the Middle Ages to the present day see P. Ariès, *Western Attitudes to Death* (M. Boyars, 1976) and *The Hour of our Death* (Allen Lane, 1981).
6 These notes on the Yolngu are based on a very graphic and detailed account by Janice Reid, 'A Time to Live, A Time to Grieve', *Culture, Medicine and Psychiatry* 3 (1979), pp. 319–46.
7 The journal *Mortality* draws upon anthropological, sociological and religious insights to give an added dimension to our understanding of death, bereavement and associated rituals.

Select Bibliography

This short bibliography includes some of the works on dying and bereavement which the authors have found particularly valuable.

Bentley J., Best A. and Hunt J. (Eds.), *Funerals, An Anthology and Guide*, Hodder & Stoughton 1994

Bluebond-Langner M., *The Private World of Dying Children*, Princeton UP 1978

Bowlby J., *Attachment and Loss Vol. iii: Loss, sadness and depression*, Penguin 1981 (a key text)

Boyd K., Higgs R. and Pinching A. (Eds.), *The New Dictionary of Medical Ethics*, British Medical Journal 1997

Doyle D., Hanks G. and MacDonald N. (Eds.), *Oxford Textbook of Palliative Medicine* (2nd edition), Oxford UP 1998

Gordon R., *Dying and Creating – A Search for Meaning*, Society for Analytical Psychology, London 1978

Green J. and Green M., *Dealing with Death: Practices and Procedures*, Chapman & Hall 1992

Harris P., *What to Do When Someone Dies*, 'Which' Books 1998

Hick J., *Death and Eternal Life*, Macmillan 1985

Hindmarch C., *On the Death of a Child*, Oxford Radcliffe 1993

Hinton J., *Dying* (2nd edition), Penguin 1972 (essential reading)

Jacobs M., *The Presenting Past*, Oxford UP 1986

Judd D., *Give Sorrow Words – working with a dying child*, Whurr 1995

Jupp P. and Rogers T., *Interpreting Death: Christian Theology and Pastoral Practice*, Cassell 1997

Kubler-Ross E., *Death – The Final Stage of Growth*, Prentice Hall 1975

Kubler-Ross E., *On Death and Dying*, Routledge 1990

Marshall F., *Losing a Parent*, Sheldon 1993

Neuberger J., *Caring for Dying People of Different Faiths*, Mosby Wolfe 1994

Parkes C. M., *Bereavement – Studies of Grief in Adult Life* (3rd edition) Penguin 1996 (essential reading)

Parkes C. M., Laungani P. and Young B., *Death and Bereavement Across Cultures*, Routledge 1997

Pincus L., *Death and the Family*, Faber & Faber 1981

Raphael B., *The Anatomy of Bereavement*, Routledge 1985

Raphael B., *When Disaster Strikes: a handbook for professionals*, Routledge 1986

Rees D. (Ed.), *Death and Bereavement: The Psychological, Religious and Cultural Interfaces*, Whurr 1996

Rinpoche S., *The Tibetan Book of Living and Dying*, HarperCollins 1993

Speck P., *Loss and Grief in Medicine*, Ballière Tindall 1978

Speck P., *Being There – pastoral care in time of illness*, SPCK 1988

Stroebe M. S., Stroebe W. and Hansson R., *Handbook of Bereavement: Theory, Research and Intervention*, Cambridge University Press 1993

Tolstoy L., *The Death of Ivan Illych*, Penguin 1989

Tschudin V., *Counselling for Loss and Bereavement*, Ballière Tindall 1996

Twycross R. (Ed.), *Mud and Stars – Reflections on the Hospice Movement*, Sobell Publications 1991

Wells R., *Helping Children Cope With Grief – Facing a Death in the Family*, Sheldon 1988

Wertheimer A., *A Special Scar: Experiences of People Bereaved by Suicide*, Routledge 1991

Worden J. W., *Grief Counselling and Grief Therapy*, (2nd edition) Routledge 1991

Index

abnormalities, congenital 54
absolution 78
accidental death 60-4
activity 68, 73-4, 122
adolescents, death of 56-9
Aderman, D. 35
after-life 137
AIDS 100-1
aims, pastoral 74
alcohol: as sedative 11; abuse 121
All Souls' Day 112
anatomical research, donation of bodies
    for 89, 102-3, 152
anger 6-8, 27, 57, 122; at suicide 55; over
    funeral arrangements 103-4; against
    God 136
anniversary of death 12, 106
anointing 80-1
Anthony, Sylvia 59
anxiety 26-30; of relatives of a dying
    person 33; about destination of the
    deceased 94, 111
appraisal 143-4
attachment and separation 15-16, 42
Augustine 110
Australian Aborigines 159-61
avoiding the dying 135
awareness 5-11, 25-32; cones of
    (diagram) 37

babies, death of 50-4, 131; abnormal 54
baptism of the dying 77-8
bargaining with God 25-6
bereavement: definition 14; of
    children 60
bereavement behaviour, normal patterns
    of tabulated 13
Bible reading with the dying 75
biographical model 14-15
bodies given for medical research 89,
    102-3, 152
body, goodness of 139
body image 47
Book of Common Prayer 74-5
Bowlby, John 14, 15-16, 41
brain stem death 85
Brandon, S. G. F. 45 n.9
Buddhism 28, 159
burial: in woodland 113; at sea 114;
    in different cultures 157

Campbell, Alastair 146
Caplan, G. 15, 44
Carkhuff, R. R. 134
certificate of death 114, 149-51
chaplains see ministers
children: how adults explain death to
    them 45; death of 56-9; concepts of
    death 59-60; last rites for dying
    children 81; viewing a dead body 88;
    attending funerals 112-13; telling
    them of someone's death 112
church (local congregation) 127
churchmanship 139
Clebsch, W. A. 43
clergy see ministers
coffins 112, 158, 160
commendatory prayer 82-4; 90-1
cones of awareness (diagram) 37
confession 78
confirmation, sacramental, for the
    dying 78
consent: to treatment 31; to
    post-mortem examination 149-51
control and decision-making 30,
    44; and medical examination 47
coping strategies 15, 58
coroners 86, 151
cot death 51, 123
cremation 159
crematorium services 101-2
crisis theory 15
Cruse Bereavement Care 12
crying 5-6
cultural patterns and customs 123, 157-61

DIY funerals 114-15
Davies, Douglas 159
death: a gradual process 73; moment of
    84; practical arrangements following
    149, 152; see also brain stem death;
    certificate of death
decision-making 30
delayed grief 119-21
denial of death 5, 25, 60, 65, 88,
    91, 121; effect upon children 59-60
depression 9-11, 32-3, 122-4
despair 124
development and growth 2, 9, 74, 124
dignity, loss of 29-30
disbelief and shock 4-5, 23-4

disasters 61-4, 122
divorce and grief 42-3, 94, 121
doubt 26
drowsiness 76
drugs 28, 76; and depression 33; abuse 121
dual-process model 15, 68

education for death 133-4
Egan, Gerard 140-1
equilibrium 15
eucharist *see* Holy Communion; requiems
eulogy 100
euthanasia 31, 34 n.5, 72
exorcism 124

faith in God in times of crisis 1-2; as 'assurance policy' 7; questioned 26
family: loss of 29-30; providing help to the bereaved 96-7
fantasy 53-4
fear: of loneliness 28-9; of loss of control 29; of pain 28-9; of the unknown 26
flooding therapy 63
forgiveness, sacrament of 78-9
Frankl, Victor 29 n.4
Freud, Sigmund 14, 40
friends: loss of 29-30; providing help to the bereaved 96-7
funeral directors 92
Funeral Ombudsman 103-4
funeral wakes 104
funerals 89-106; place in grief process 12; for stillborn babies 87; secular 113-15

God, people's attitude to in crisis 1-2; bargaining with 25-6; people's images of 132
graves on private land 113-14
grave goods 114, 158-9
gravestones 109
'green' funerals 113-15
grief 65-8; definition 1, 14; resolution of 11-12; prolonged 11, 121-2; classification of 'normal' grief 13; models and theories of 12-15; for impending loss 23, 73; and madness 40, 119, 120; public 105-6, 116, 160-1; delayed 119-21
grief work: model 14; encouraged by funeral 95-6
growth and development 2, 9, 74, 124
guidance 74, 92
guilt 8-9; of parents at death of a baby 52-3; of mourners 94-5

handicapped children 54
headstones 109
healing, ministry of 81
healing centres 25
heaven 138

helping 96-7; model of 140-1
Hinduism 102, 159
Hinton, John 129
Holy Communion 79-80, 112; *see also* requiems
hope 26-7, 138
hospices ix, 147-8; for children 58-9
hospital chaplains *see* ministers
hypochondriasis 125

identification, relationship based on 124-5
images of God 132
incorporation 104-9
inquests 151
Islam and bodies of dead people 85-6, 88
isolation 10

Jaekle, C. R. 43
Judaism: and bodies of dead people 85-6, 88, 159; structured mourning period 105-6

Kubler-Ross, Elizabeth 14, 25, 34-5, 135

Lampe, Geoffrey 138
last rites *see* anointing
lay visitors 133
laying on of hands 80-1
laying out 84-5
learning from the dying 131-2
learning theory 15
Lewis, E. 120
life after death 137
listening 10, 47, 72; at a pre-funeral visit 93-4
living wills 30
loneliness, fear of 28
loss 27-8; causing depression 33

McKinnon, Donald 138
madness 40, 119, 120
magic 53, 77, 158
marriage: death-bed 81-2; after death of a previous spouse 106; psychological principles and effect on bereavement behaviour 124-5
medical model 14
medical research, donation of bodies for 89, 102-3, 152
memorials 109
memories 65-8
mentally handicapped people 102
ministers 129-46; role of ix, 9, 25; people's expectations of 7-8, 71-2, 129-30; role prior to a death 71-3; as representatives of God 8, 133; role in funeral service 98-9; as representing faith 130; support for 127, 142-4; personal beliefs of 134-5
miscarriage 52, 87
Moody, Raymond 36

mourning: definition 14; structured period 105–6, 116, 160–1; pathological 125
myths surrounding death and burial 157–61

naming and blessing of babies 77
near death experiences 36–8, 159
Niebuhr, Reinhold 30
non-Christians, funerals for 102, 159

Ombudsman 103–4
organ transplants 32, 85–6, 152, 153

pain 28–9
palliative care 148
Parkes, C. M. 14
pastoral aims 74
performance reviews 143–4
persistent vegetative state 31
pets 45, 103
phase model 14
physical appearance, changes in 47
Pincus, Lily 123
pining 6
post-funeral visit 106–9
post-mortem examinations 88–9, 149–51
postponed grief 119–21
post-traumatic stress disorder 15, 62
prayer: for serenity 30, 84; with the dying 76; of commendation 82–4, 90–1; at a pre-funeral visit 93; as protection from relationships 93, 135; by the bereaved 107; for the dead 109–12
preaching 100–1, 137
pregnancy and delayed mourning 120
problems of grief 119–28
projection, relationship based on 124–5
prolongation of grief 11, 121–2
propitiation 158
psychiatric illness: resulting from failure to grieve earlier 120; causing later denial 121
psychiatric referral 127
psycho-analytic theory 15
purgatory, doctrine of 110

Raphael-Leff, Joan 53
reaction formation 135
recollection 65–8
reconciliation 74–5, 78
Rees, Dewi 159
registration of death 149–51
regression 42
reincarnation 28, 137, 157, 159
reparation 158
requiems 95, 99, 110–12
resolution of grief 11–12, 32–6, 105
resurrection 99, 137–9
resuscitation 31–2, 86
rites of passage 70–1, 139–40

ritual 158; function of 70–1; prior to death 71–3; following death 89–115

sacraments 77–81
sadness 10, 33; compared with clinical depression 123
Schulz, R. 35
secular funerals 113–15
sedation 11
Selby, Peter 138
self-help groups 108, 125, 126
separation 28; and funeral rites 90–2, 160
serenity 30, 73, 84
sermons 137; in the funeral service 100–1
services: memorial 103; *see also* funerals; sacraments
shock and disbelief 4–5, 23–4
shrines 125
Sikhism 159
sleep by the dying person 33, 76
Smith, JoAnn Kelly 35
sorrow 1
spiritualism 91
stillbirth 7, 50–4, 86–7
stillness 73
stoicism 107
Stroebe, M. S. & W. 15, 68
sudden infant death 51, 123
suffering, fear of 28–9
suicide 31, 54–6, 122

telling children of someone's death 112
telling patients their prognosis 136
thanksgiving for the life of the deceased 95
Thompson, Melvyn 132
Tillich, Paul 9
tombstones 109
transference 140
transition 94–6
Truax, C. B. 134
trust: during loss 40–1; in God 41

unction 80–1

van Gennep, Arnold 70
viaticum 79–80
victims of disaster 62, 122
Victoria, Queen 123
viewing the body 87–8
visits by clergy, pre-funeral 92–4; post-funeral 106–9
visits by laity 108
volunteers 129, 133

wakes 104
Walter, T. 14–15
Williams, H. A. 44, 138
wills 30, 82, 149
Wilson, Michael 147
woodland burials 113–15
Worden, J. W. 12 n.6, 16

Yolngu people 159–61